AQUA APOCALYPSES

CASE STUDIES BASED ON DISASTERS RELATED TO
WATER RESOURCE MANAGEMENT

SONALI BHANDARI

AQUA APOCALYPSES

CASE STUDIES BASED DISASTERS RELATED TO

WATER RESOURCE MANAGEMENT

Copyright © 2018 by Sonali Bhandari

First Printing, 2018

ISBN: 1982072423

ISBN-13: 978-1982072421

Cover Design by SONALI BHANDARI

Printed in the United States of America

TO MY PARENTS

CONTENTS

LIST OF ILLUSTRATIONS

LIST OF TABLES

ABBREVIATIONS

Av.	Average
Approx.	approximately
AC	Alternating Current
APELL	Awareness and Preparedness for Emergencies at the Local Level
BHN	Bombay High North
BOD	Biological Oxygen Demand
BNHS	Bombay Natural History Society
BSI	Botanical Survey of India
BTEX	Benzene, Toluene, Ethylbenzene, Xylenes
CEE	Center for Environment Education
BVIEER	Bhartiya Vidyapeeth University's Institute of Environment Education and Research
CERCLA	Comprehensive Environment Response, Compensation and Liability Act
Corp.	Corporation
CPR Chennai	Chetpat Pattabhirama Ramaswami Chennai
CSE	Center for Science and Environment
DC	Direct Current
DDT	Dichloro Diphenyl Trichloroethane
DO	Dissolved Oxygen
EDA	Emergency Declaration Area

EPA	Environment Protection Agency
EE	Environmental Education
EEZ	Exclusive Economic Zone
ESI	Environment Sensitivity Index
FO	Fuel Oil
FFO	Furnace Fuel Oil
FC	*Faecal coliform*
FRY	Federal Republic of Yugosla*via*
GIS	Geographic Information System
HO	Heavy Oil
ICPDR	International Commission for the Protection of the Danube River
ICSU	International Council for Science
IMO	International Maritime Organization
JNPT	Jawarharlal Nehru Port Trust
KL	Kilo litres
L	Litres
LCARA	Love Canal Area Revitalization Agency
lbs	Pounds
m^3	Cubic meters
MPT	Mumbai Port Trust

MPCB	Mumbai Pollution Control Board
MV	Motor Vessel
MT	Motor Tanker
MS	Motor Ship
ND	Not Detectable
NEERI	National Environmental Engineering Research Institute
NIO	National Institute of Oceanography
NOAA	National Oceanic and Atmospheric Administration
NGO	Non Government Organization
NM	Nautical Miles
NW	North West
OCHA	United Nations Office for the Coordination of Humanitarian Affairs
ONGC	Oil and Natural Gas Corporation
Pt.	Port
PHC	Petroleum Hydrocarbons
P.L.	Public Law
P.M.T.	Pilipinas Micro-matrix Technology
SACON	Salim Ali Center for Ornithology and Natural History
SBM	Single Buoy Mooring
SKO	Superior kerosene oil
SS	Soluble Solids

S	South
SW	South West
TC	*Coliform bacteria*
TCDD	Tetra chloro dibenzo dioxine
TERI	The Energy and Resources Institute
TVC	Total *Via*ble Count
UNDP	United Nations Development Programme
UNEP	United Nations Environment Programme
UN/ECE	United Nations Economic Commission For Europe
UKSN	Uttarakhand Seva Nidhi
US	United States
42 U.S.C.	US code dealing with public health, social welfare and civil rights
USGS	United States Geological Survey
W.D.N.Y.	Western District of New York
WII	Wildlife Institute of India
WWF	World Wildlife Fund
ZSI	Zoological Survey of India

PREFACE

In the spring semester of 2013, I was teaching the compulsory University Grants Commission prescribed 'Environmental Studies' course. As part of assessment for this course, students had to submit projects on a given topic. Since there were only fourteen students in my class, each student was assigned an independent environment-related project topic. Students were required to conduct a thorough literature search for their respective topics and submit a report followed by a presentation. The project reports I received inspired me to put this book together.

Among the various assigned topics, I decided to focus on case studies on disasters related to water resource management. Two of these case studies - Love Canal and Minimata Disease - are based on events that occurred in First world countries. The seeds for both events were sown at the end of the nineteenth century, although repercussions were felt decades later and it took a few more decades for the full-scale of the disasters to be realized and dealt with. Both events are excellent illustrations of the principles of *sustainability* and *sustainable development* and demonstrate how essential it is in the contemporary world to develop a keen sensitivity towards the environment lest mankind has to face unpredictable and dangerous backlashes of nature.

The other two case studies - Baia Mare and Mumbai Oil Spill - were more recent occurrences. Both happened in developing countries and illustrate how localized events can have widespread and varied impact on nature and human society. Both disasters are a measure of the quantum of progress made in handling such incidences while bringing to light areas that need to be developed.

Through an elaborate discussion of selected case studies, this book is an endeavor to raise environmental awareness and education among students, particularly, at the undergraduate level and instill sensitivity, values and moral responsibility towards Mother Earth.

ACKNOWLEDGMENTS

I would like to thank all my students for the wonderful project reports they submitted – Khushboo Bano, Nisha Chaudhury, Surapaneni Meghana, Vishal Shakya, Akshat Arora, Kaustabh S. Kambekar, Saksham, Padarthi Sindhuja, Padarthi Sindhuratna, Revati Ramesan, Krishnabhamini Sinha, and Ankit Dwivedi.

I would like to thank my family for their constant support and encouragement during preparation of this manuscript. Finally, I would like to acknowledge my niece and nephew for suggesting a title for this book.

1 INTRODUCTION

"To see a World in a Grain of Sand
And a Heaven in a Wild Flower,
Hold Infinity in the palm of your hand
And Eternity in an hour."

William Blake, Auguries of Innocence

I.1   ENVIRONMENTAL AWARENESS IN ANCIENT INDIA

ENVIRONMENTAL AWARENESS and concern in the Indian sub-continent is as old as the dawn of its civilization. The ancient Vedas, Puranas and Upanishads are repositories of knowledge, culmination of ancient Indian wisdom and genesis of most of the modern disciplines. [1-9] Indeed there is hardly any field of study – physics, mathematics, astronomy, literature, grammar, alternate medicine, philosophy, yoga, music *etc.*- whose foundation cannot be tracked down to the Vedas. Needless to say that they contain several references to environmental protection, ecological balance, weather cycles, and the hydrological cycle. [10] Our wise Seers fully recognized the harmful effects of environmental deterioration caused naturally or anthropogenically. People in Vedic times regarded Nature and the Environment in a holistic manner and considered living in harmony with nature as a way of life.

I.1.1 BIOSPHERE AND THE ENVIRONMENT

The Vedas emphasized the need to protect the environment, which encompassed protecting the Earth (*Prithvi*), Heavens (*Dyaus*) and everything that lies in between- the atmosphere and the environment (*Paryavaran*). [10] *Rigveda* mentions deities like *Mitra*[1], *Varuna*[2], *Indra*[3], *Maruts*[4] and *Aditya*[5] as the ones who have been assigned the task of maintaining balance among the various components of Nature. Seers conceded that indiscriminate anthropogenic activities would result in imbalances in seasons, rainfall pattern, crops and atmosphere and deteriorate the quality of air, water and earth. There are many hymns seeking the blessings of the five gross elements or *panchbhoota* of Nature- *akash* or sky; *vayu* or air; *agni* or fire; *apah* or water and *prithvi* or earth. [11] People were careful about preserving Nature's bounties and refrained from activities that could cause them harm.

It is interesting to note that the *Rigveda* clearly mentions the presence of a protective layer that filters the harmful rays of the Sun and protects the Earth, while praising the radiation that enters the Earth. All four major Vedas emphasize the importance of maintaining the delicate balance between the season's cycles. This balance is likely to get altered due to climactic change triggered by indiscriminate anthropogenic activities.

---

[1] In the Rigveda, *Mitra* is indistinguishable from *Varuna* and the two form the pair- *Mitra-Varuna*. The pair, however, essentially has the same characteristics as *Varuna* alone. In the *Atharveda*, *Mitra* is associated with sunrise.

[2] *Varuna* is the lord of *Rita*, the universal natural order. He is sovereign God, great King, law-maker and ruler of cosmos and even of the Gods.

[3] *Indra* is the most powerful God who frees *Vritra*- the symbol of clouds to free water

[4] *Maruts* are *Indra*'s associates

[5] *Aditya* in the singular means Sun-God, *Surya*; the *Bhagavata purana* lists 12 *Adityas* as twelve Sun-Gods; a different *Aditya* shines in every month of the year

Living in harmony with Nature and the Cosmic Order seemed to be the prevailing theme in all aspects of living during Vedic times. Whether it was building a city or a house or a temple or for curing and treating diseases, the approach was always subtle, scientific, holistic and the guiding principle was always to seek similarities with the laws of Nature.

I.1.2   ARCHITECTURE AND THE ENVIRONMENT

The ancient science of *Sthapatya Veda* gives extensive description of life supporting building and design principles. [12]   The word *Sthapatya* means establishment and *Veda* means knowledge.   *Sthapatya Veda*, therefore, means the knowledge of establishing a relationship between the owner, house and the cosmic order. Seers believed that the Universe was in perfect order since its inception. If an architect can establish a good relationship between the building and the Universe, the lives of the residents will be blissful, creative and healthier.

Design principles established in the *Sthapatya Veda* were also used widely in temple construction. There are precise mathematical and astrological calculations, proportions of building plans, specific orientation and applied knowledge of subtle physical properties, that together contributed to the feeling of spiritual content.

I.1.3.   MEDICINE AND THE ENVIRONMENT

Even the earlier Vedas recognized the curative powers of various elements of Nature *viz.* air, water and the Sun. *Rigveda X. 168.4* prayed *"O Vayu (Air), bring your medicines and do away with all ailments because you are the only one who is full of curative powers."*[5] *Yajurveda XXXIII.92* praises the functions of the Sun *"Just as the Sun, set in Heaven, the benefactor of humanity, increasing in power on Earth, ripens medicines and grows food, removes darkness of night with his luster, shines forth, so should ye dispel ignorance………..".* [5] *Samveda 1638* venerates the role of Water as a source of life, *"O Water! Let your most prosperous juice be ministered to us in this world with the readiness that affectionate mothers apply to their infants"*. [5] The next hymn highlights the role of water in healing diseases. It is noteworthy that the role of water as medicine was known to them and therefore, it became more essential to keep water clean or pollution-free. The *Yajurveda* describes elaborate rituals to pacify the *panchbhootas* (the five elements of Nature) for the purpose of healing both the Cosmic being and the individual soul.

However, it is only the Ayurveda that gives comprehensive cures and treatments for various diseases and ailments. [12] Ayurveda is a subsection of the *Atharveda*, the last of the four Vedas composed between 3000 BC and 2000 BC, and is an umbrella text comprising of various disciplines including *Kayachikitsa* (Internal Medicine), *Shalakya Tantra* (thoracic surgery, ophthalmology and otolaryngology), *Shalya Tantra* (Surgery), *Agada Tantra* (Toxicology), *Bhuta Vidya* (Psychiatry), *Kaumarabhritya* (Pediatrics), *Rasayana* (rejuvenation or anti-aging), *Vajikarana* (the science of fertility). The underlying principle behind Ayurvedic prescriptions is striking a balance between Man and Nature by identifying similarities between laws of Nature and functioning of the human body. A wide variety of methods are used for curing and treating in Ayurveda like, yoga (meditation), aromatherapy, gems, precious stones, amulets, herbs, diet, color and surgery. Each of these methods of treatment has a direct connection with the natural eco-systems surrounding us.

I.2 ENVIRONMENTAL AWARENESS IN THE CONTEMPORARY GLOBAL SCENE

In the western world, the literary giants of the Romantic era in the early nineteenth century expressed their concern for the environment in their writings. The British poet William Wordsworth travelled widely in the Lake District and wrote that "it is a sort of national property in which every man has a right and interest who has an eye to perceive and a heart to enjoy."[13] With the advent of the Industrial Revolution in the mid-eighteenth century, time and again voices were raised against air pollution, water pollution, and unhygienic living conditions in cities. Systematic efforts with respect to the environment only began in Great Britain in the late nineteenth century with the formation of the Commons Preservation Society in 1865. [14] The Society fought for rural preservation against encroachments of industrialization. In the United States, environmental campaigns began in the late 19th century mainly to protect natural resources of the West with thinkers like John Muir [15] and Henry David Thoreau making key philosophical contributions [16]. Thoreau documented his experiences in his book, *Walden,* where he argued people should come close to nature. [17]

In the post-war era, the landmark event that gave birth to contemporary 'Environmentalism' was the book called '*Silent Spring*' written by American biologist Rachel Carson in 1962. [18] This book questioned the indiscriminate use of DDT (Dichloro Diphenyl Trichloroethane) and release of such large amounts of chemicals into the atmosphere without fully understanding their impact. The book also described the movement of DDT, known as the miracle compound, up in the food chain and how it caused severe damage to humans. DDT was a widely used pesticide at that time and in the early 1920s, its discovery led to bumper food production. Carson's findings created a furor in the United States and President John F. Kennedy had to set up a committee to investigate Carson's findings. The book generated greater awareness and interest in society about environmental problems such as air pollution and oil spills. Environmental concerns found their voice in pressure groups. Most conspicuous among them were '*Greenpeace*' [19] and '*Friends of the Earth*' [20].

Almost a decade later came the papers of Barbara Ward and Rene Dubois in 1972 called '*Only One Earth*'. [21] Their research was funded by UNDP (United Nations Development Program) and highlighted the conflict between the biosphere of Man's inheritance and the techno-sphere of His creation. The main conclusion of the study was that there was a need to strike a balance between economic growth and sustainable development. The *'Club of Rome'* funded by independent scientists also expressed similar concerns and proposed almost identical schemes for the survival of mankind on this planet. [22] Another attempt to voice concern about the rapidly deteriorating Earth's environment was a research finding called *'Limits to Growth'* published in 1972 based on data collected at the global level on a mathematical model. [23] The model predicted a very dark future and stated that continued resource shortages, overcrowding, pollution, famines *etc.* will soon control current trends in population growth, natural resource exploitation, and capital investment in agriculture. The model met with heavy criticism.

Another milestone to raise global environmental awareness was achieved with the creation of *Earth Day*. [24] Earth Day was first observed on 21st March, 1970 in San Francisco and other cities in the United States. *March 21 also coincides with the first day of Spring.* The United Nation's first major international conference on environmental issues was held from 5th to 12th June, 1972 and was called the *United Nations Conference on the Human Environment (also called the Stockholm conference)*. This conference became the turning point in international development politics. [25]

Gaia: A new look at life on Earth published by James Lovelock in 1979 advocated the *Gaia* hypothesis. [26] This theory proposed that life on earth can be understood as a single organism and this became an important part of the Deep Green ideology. Throughout the rest of the history of environmentalism, there have been back and forth debates on radical followers of *Deep Green ideology* and more mainstream environmentalists.

Since the 1980s, increasing concern about *global warming* and *climate change* has brought to the forefront environmental issues forcing greater public debate and discussion. And since the 2000s, this concern has spread to include other issues like *ozone hole, El Nino, overpopulation, deforestation* and *genetic engineering.*

I.3   ENVIRONMENTAL EDUCATION IN CONTEMPORARY INDIA

In colonial times, the first attempt to introduce environmental education into the curriculum was initiated by Mahatama Gandhi in 1937 in a movement called *'Nai Taleem'* of Basic Education. [27] The aim was to generate *"reflective learners, skilled with useful knowledge, who were integrated into community life through engagement in productive work and who desired to undertake service for humanity".* [2] This movement remained at the evolutionary stage and was never fully implemented. It came to a grinding halt with India's independence and Gandhi's assassination in 1948. Since then, learning has been replaced by current conventional models based on colonial methodologies of thinking, learning by rote techniques and lack of encouragement of free thinking. Living in harmony with nature has been a part of the Indian tradition and was long publicized by Gandhi through his *Basic Education Program.* However, environmental education was formally introduced into the Indian schooling system as a result of the *Kothari Commission's recommendation* (1964-1966). Another major impetus to environmental education came with the establishment of the *Center for Environmental Education* in 1984, that pioneered several movements for incorporating and integrating environmental education at all grade levels within the school system. The *Supreme Court mandates* in 1991 and 2003 led to the formation of national policy, that led to making changes in *National Curriculum Framework* (National Commission for Education Research and Technology, 2005) and *National Council of Teacher Educators'* new curriculum for teacher educators (National Council of Teacher Educators, 2005).

The liberalization of the Indian economy in the 1990s catalyzed the pace of growth in all sectors of the economy. In the current global scenario, India is the second fastest growing economy in the world. This rapid development has raised concerns for protection of the environment and fast depleting natural resources. [3, 28] Table 1 summarizes key developments in environment education in India post-independence. [29]

Bhartiya Vidyapeeth University's Institute of Environment Education and Research (BVIEER) and *Center for Environment Education* (CEE) have made laudable efforts in educating teachers. Since its formation in 1984, CEE has worked tirelessly to publicize environmental education with teachers in governmental and Non-Governmental Organizations. It has established regional centers, functioning as resource centers for school students, teachers and teacher educators. CEE can also be given credit for publishing India's first journal in the field- *Journal of Education for Sustainable Development*. It is also important to highlight the role of NGOs working in this field. The 2008-2009 WWF directory of environmental NGOs in India lists 2342 such organizations working in diverse environment-related fields from nature to water conservation to biodiversity protection to promoting environmental policies. [30] All these programs promote environmentalism while keeping in mind the religious sentiments of people. For instance, in western India, traditional clay/plaster of paris Ganesha idols prepared during Ganesha festival have been replaced by eco-friendly idols made of straw, mud, paper and other biodegradable materials, that do not cause water pollution when immersed in water bodies at the end of festivities [31].

Besides, there are several well-known non-governmental and governmental organizations that are spreading the cause of environmental awareness and protection. [32] Two most prominent NGOs are *Bombay Natural History Society* (BNHS) and *World Wildlife Fund* (WWF). BNHS started as a small society formed by six members in 1883.

Starting from a group of *shikaris*[6] it has grown into a major organization that has effectively influenced environmental conservation policy in India. WWF began in 1969 in Mumbai but later shifted its headquarters to Delhi. It has several branch offices all over Delhi. It propagates wildlife education and awareness and works as a think tank and lobby force for environment and development issues. The *Center for Science and Environment* (CSE), New Delhi, organizes environmental campaigns, workshops and conferences and produces several popular environment-related publications. The *CPR Environment Education Center*, Chennai, was set up in 1988 and works on spreading public awareness regarding environment conservation, with a particular focus on NGOs, teachers, women, youth and children. The *Uttarakhand Seva Nidhi* (UKSN), Almora is a Nodal Agency that acts as a fund giving organization to NGOs. Its major focus is to train school teachers. *Kalpvriksh, Pune* works from Pune on a variety of fronts- education and awareness, investigation and research, direct action and lobbying, and litigation with regard to environment and development issues. The *Salim Ali Center for Ornithology and Natural History* (SACON), Coimbatore supports a group of dedicated scientists whose work focuses on studying the 'threatened biodiversity' of the country. *Wildlife Institute of India* (WII), Dehradun was established in 1982 as a major training establishment for Forest Officials and Research in Wildlife Management. It trains personnel in eco-development, wildlife biology, habitat management and Nature interpretation. Over the years, it has added an enormous amount of information on India's biological wealth. The *Botanical Survey of India* (BSI) was established in 1890 at the Royal Botanic Gardens, Calcutta. It was shut down in 1939 and re-opened in 1954. The BSI has currently nine regional offices all over India and conducts surveys of plant resources in different regions. The *Zoological Survey of India* (ZSI) was established in

---

[6] A game hunter

1916 and its objective was to conduct a systematic survey of fauna in India. The previous collections from the Asiatic Society of Bengal between 1814 and 1875 and the Indian Museum in Calcutta between 1875 and 1916 were transferred to the ZSI. It currently operates from 16 regional centers and has achieved milestones in the fields of taxonomy and ecology.

Over the centuries, there has been a major change in attitude towards the environment in the Indian sub-continent. The ancient Indian ideologies of "Karma" and "Nirvana" or salvation have been replaced by 'materialism' and 'economic development'. Attaining fulfillment through simple living has been replaced by glorification of 'affluence'. Globalization means the current generation is exposed to more 'choices' and, also have the economic means to satisfy those options. [33] Sages and Seers held higher status than rulers as education was more esteemed than power in ancient India. In today's India, this principle has just been reversed. There is strong emphasis on the individual's "everyday behavioral change, rather than an actual connection to and affinity with the environment (be it people, nature and/or animals)". [34] Environmental preservation is important but not at the cost of development. Living in harmony with the Cosmos has been substituted by 'sustainability' and 'sustainable development'. [35]

Table 1: Chronology of Key Events in Environmental Education in India[29]

Year	Achievement	Implication
1964-66	Report of the Education Commission - the Kothari Commission	Considered the root of Environmental Education (EE) in India
1975	Approach for Curriculum for the Ten-Year School: and a framework for Curriculum for the Ten-Year School	First framework to explicitly indicate teaching of EE
1984 *1986*	Establishment of the Center of Environment Education (CEE) as a National Center for Excellence in EE under Ministry of Environment and Forests Adoption of the National Policy on Education The national Environmental Awareness Campaign of the Ministry of Environment and Forests	CEE worked with different sectors- particularly education- to spread environmental awareness. First National Policy that indicated EE to be included in schools.
1988-89	Environmental Orientation to School Education Scheme of the Ministry of Human Resources Development	Called for orientating curriculum to include EE

Table 1: Chronology of Key Events in Environmental Education in India (Contd.)

Year	Achievements	Implication
1989	C.P.R. Chennai established as a second Center of Excellence	Works towards promoting EE in South India
1991	First Supreme Court of India mandate requiring the University Grants Commission to prescribe courses on the environment at all levels of higher education	The judiciary steps in to help control environmental problems- a first of its kind step
2003	Second Supreme Court judgment mandating EE to be taught across all formal education institutions	Requires every school in every state of India to teach EE
2005	National Council for Teacher Education provides the EE curriculum framework for teachers and teacher educators National Curriculum Framework clearly specifying the role of EE is drafted.	A major step providing national level impetus for the inclusion of EE in teacher education. School curriculum now includes EE and has to be mandatorily taught.

I.4   BACKGROUND

In order to illustrate the concepts of 'sustainability' and 'sustainable development', projects were assigned to students as part of the UGC-recommended compulsory 'Environment Studies' course at the Undergraduate level. The nature of Environmental Studies is such that practical instruction is inherent to the subject and self-study is one of the best ways to motivate students to learn and inspire them to become responsible, environmentally aware global citizens. Project topics were assigned to students on global issues though based on concepts or terms taught in class. In the following chapters, few global case studies on water resource management have been discussed.

Chapter 2 is about how a quiet and picturesque prefecture in Japan opened its doors to a chemical company, which initially manufactured carbide-based fertilizers. As Japan's imperialistic might flourished, the technological prowess of the company bloomed. With the advent of new high pressure gas technology, the company started manufacturing acetaldehyde and related compounds. This process required a Mercury catalyst and as a result, generated toxic Mercury-laden waste. All this waste was dumped in the nearby bay. Soon, fish, cats and eventually human beings began to exhibit 'strange' symptoms. This led to the discovery of the most dangerous pollution-related diseases in Japan and the world.

Chapter 3 discusses how Aurul Company (a joint collaboration between an Australian company and the Romanian Government) started processing an old, contaminated tailings dam by extracting residual gold and silver from previously extracted processes. Large quantity of cyanide was required to extract gold and silver. After gold extraction, the tailings fluid was pumped to the new Aurul pond 6.5 km away through a pipeline. In January 2000, excess precipitation led to a breakage in the Aurul tailings dam and the cyanide-contaminated water spilt into the Sasar River, then into Lapus River before joining the Somes River. The cyanide plume then flowed into the Tisza River and eventually, down into the River Danube. The three most affected countries by this incident were Romania, Hungary and Federal Republic of Yugoslavia. The chapter then discusses the environmental impact caused by such a large-scale disaster.

Chapter 4 describes how a canal dug at the end of the nineteenth century for the purposes of enhancing hydroelectric power supply in Niagara Falls County, U.S.A., was abandoned and became a dumping ground for hazardous and toxic waste. Over the years, settlements and schools came up above the landfill site oblivious to the danger lying underneath. The chapter then goes on to describe how the landfill site was re-discovered and its various consequences and repercussions.

Chapter 5 is about the collision of two cargo ships-MSC Chitra and MV Khalija III- near Mumbai in 2010 and the resultant oil spill caused by the accident in the marine waters and beaches. Management and environmental impact of oil spills in general and the specific consequences of the Mumbai 2010 Oil Spill on water quality, sediments and flora and fauna have been discussed. In addition, clean-up of oil spills in general and the indigenous technology employed for cleaning up after the Mumbai 2010 Oil Spill have been further explained.

2 MINIMATA DISEASE

'When we try to pick out anything by itself, we find it hitched to everything else in the Universe'

John Muir

II.1   INTRODUCTION

THE AREA around Minimata Bay in the Yatsushiro Sea (the Sea of mysterious fire) of Kumamoto Prefecture, Japan, was known for its beauty, fishing boats, lush green rice paddy fields and groves of orange trees (see Fig. 1). [1, 2, 3 and 4] The picturesque sea was also endowed with a natural fish reef that served as a spawning site for numerous species of fish. However, in the 1950s, a perplexing phenomenon surfaced in the town. Shellfish began to die; fish floated on the surface of water and were washed ashore; seaweeds ceased to grow; cats danced on the streets and suddenly dropped dead; and dead birds dropped from the air. Around the mid-1950s abnormal behavior was observed among human beings too- friends or family members shouted in a frenzied manner; slurred their speech; or suddenly dropped their chopsticks at dinner. These were the beginning of birth pangs of one of the worst cases of industrial pollution in Japan.

Fig. 1: The Shiranui Sea (or the Yatsushiro Sea) is an inland sea surrounded by Kyushu and the Amakusa Islands. It covers an area of nearly 1,400 km^2 (about the size of Lake Biwa, Honshu, Japan), 6 to 16 km East to West, and 70 km North to South. On average it is about 50 m in depth, but the range of ebb and flow is 4 m. The coast of the southern part of the Shiranui Sea, where Minamata is located, is ragged with many inlets and coves suitable for the spawning grounds of fish and shellfish. A great variety of creatures live in this area. [5]

II.2 MINIMATA DISEASE

Minimata also referred to as Chisso-Minimata is a disease of the Central Nervous System and is caused by severe *Mercury poisoning*. [3,6 and 7] It is neither air- nor water-borne nor is it transmitted through food contamination. It is also not a genetically inherited disease. Minimata disease is caused by the consumption of fish and shellfish contaminated with methyl mercury compounds. A *congenital* form of the disease can also attack fetuses in wombs and victims are born with conditions resembling cerebral palsy. This occurs when the mother consumes seafood contaminated with methyl mercury during pregnancy and the fetus is contaminated *via* the placenta.

Symptoms of Minimata disease include sensory disorders in the distal portion of the four extremities[7]; ataxia[8]; concentric constriction of the visual field[9]; hearing impairment; disequilibrium[10]; speech impediments including blurred and unclear speech; trembling of hands and feet; and chaotic ocular movement[11] as illustrated in Fig. 2. Extreme cases can be fatal prior to insanity, paralysis and coma within weeks of inception of symptoms. In mild cases, the disease manifests itself with symptoms such as mild headache, chronic fatigue, and an inability to differentiate taste and smell.

---

[7]   loss of sensation in the hands and feet
[8]   difficulty in coordination movement of hands and feet
[9]   narrowing of the field of vision
[10] impairment of faculties for maintaining balance
[11] eye movement becomes erratic

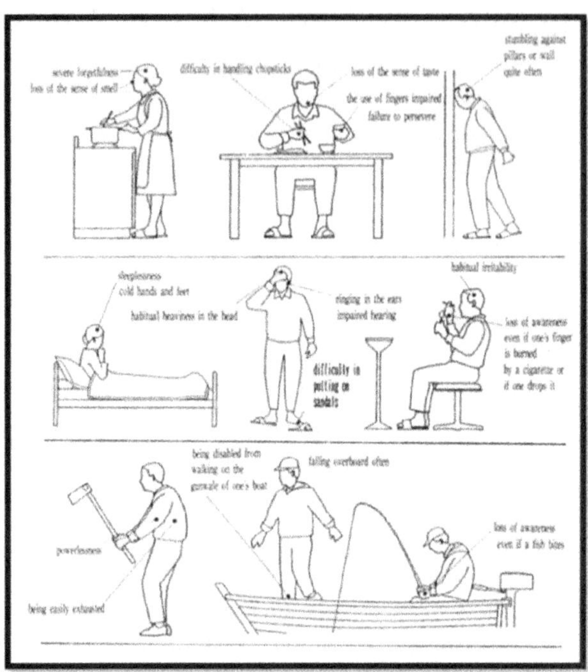

Fig. 2: The disabilities and pains caused by Minamata Disease have profound implications for the patient's daily life: outwardly invisible disabilities, such as numbness or headaches, pose more than physical problems. For example, if the patient takes rest from his work or takes a day off owing to headaches, he is likely to be branded as a lazy dog. Including such exposure to social injustices, there is no limit to the pains caused by Minamata Disease. [8]

II.3   OUTBREAK OF MINIMATA DISEASE AND GEOGRAPHICAL LOCATIONS

The first official occurrence of Minimata disease took place around Minimata Bay in Kumamoto Prefecture, in Kyushu, southernmost island of Japan in 1956. [7, 9] Strange behavior and in extreme cases, death, was observed in cats, dogs, pigs and humans for approximately thirty-six years.

In June 1965, similar symptoms were discovered among several fishermen in the lower reaches of Agano River, in the suburbs of Niigata City, in Niigata Prefecture. This was the second occurrence of Minimata disease. Since the second Minimata disease was recognized at an earlier stage, contamination was contained promptly. Despite controlling the rapid spread of the disease, there were five deaths and twenty six affected persons. [9]

In May 1973, a 'third case of Minimata disease' was reported in Ariakecho, Saga Prefecture, in Kyushu. Here also affected people were discovered in areas far away from the original pollution sources. [9]

The *original Minimata disease* and the *Niigata outbreak* are considered two of the *four big pollution related diseases* that hit Japan. The other two are *Itai-itai disease* caused due to Cadmium poisoning by Mitsui Mining and Smelting Corporation that occurred in Toyama Prefecture in 1912 and the other is *Yokkaichi Asthma* caused by Sulphur dioxide pollution from Yokkaichi in Mie Prefecture in 1961. [10]

II.4 EVENTS THAT LED TO THE FIRST OUTBREAK OF MINIMATA DISEASE

In the beginning of the twentieth century, Minimata was a small fishing and farming village, which also produced salt. [9] It was in 1908 that a young college-educated electrical engineer, Jun Noguchi, established a carbide plant in the village. This was the beginning of Chisso Corporation in Minimata Bay, 'Chisso' in Japanese means Nitrogen. Under the pretext of industrial restructuring, Japan's high economic growth policies based on utilization of cheap labor had already been initiated with the establishment of the Chisso Plant. The main use of carbide as a light source is in night fishing. Since the demand for carbide was low, sales were not high enough. The company then started to obtain Calcium cyanamide from carbide, which was further used to produce metamorphic Ammonium sulfate to be used as agricultural fertilizer.

The company began making profits with the advent of the First World War, when import of fertilizers was halted and Chisso began to monopolize the domestic market. In the years after the war, new high-pressure gas technology was introduced to synthesize Ammonium sulfate and the company began to expand into Korea to enhance Japan's colonization efforts.

In 1930 Japan's chemical industry started production of chemical compounds derived from Calcium carbide generated acetylene. [9] *Acetylene was blown over Mercuric sulfate to produce acetaldehyde by picking up one molecule of water (see Fig. 3).* Chisso began to manufacture not only acetaldehyde but also *acetic acid, ethyl acetate, cellulose acetate, vinyl acetylene, acetone, butanol, and isooctane. Through research and development in Organic Chemistry, Chisso company's chemical engineering level also became very advanced.* Such scientific and technical achievements were made possible by the highly trained labor force. Only the best engineering graduates from the Department of Engineering at Tokyo Imperial University were employed. Similarly, stringent criteria were used to hire regular staff. Through the pre- and post-Second World War periods, Japan's industrial strength was built upon *high quality low paid workers.*

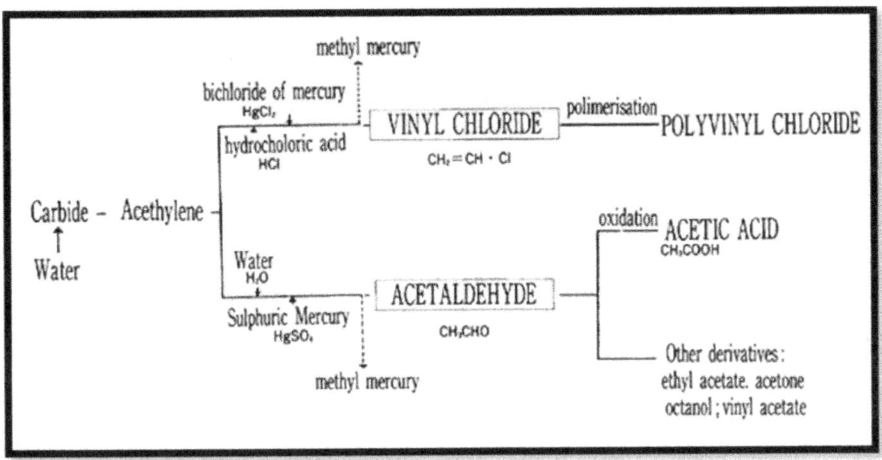

Fig. 3: Sulfuric mercury was used at Chisso, Minamata, as a catalyst in producing acetaldehyde, the material for synthetic acetic acid. In this process, the inorganic sulfuric mercury became organic; that is, methyl mercury was produced. Mercury is well-known for its high toxicity, but when it is methylated, its ability to combine with protein is enhanced and thus its toxicity is highly increased. Methyl mercury smells like a rotten egg as it evaporates directly from its crystals. [11]

As the Second World War approached, energy for aeronautics and petroleum derived products became important to the military. [9]   As Japan lacked natural petroleum resources, the only alternatives that could be provided were by acetylene chemistry-based organic products. *Acetaldehyde was a key raw material and Chisso was well advanced in the field of acetylene chemistry.* In 1941, the Minimata plant successfully started the production of *vinyl chloride plasticizer* that required a high level of acetylene chemistry. *All the waste products from the manufacture of various products were dumped without treatment into the Minimata bay that resulted in destruction of its fishery resources.*

Chisso lost 80 percent of its overseas assets after the Second World War. [9] *However, from the ashes, the Minimata complex with its long standing tradition of high technology combined with its Samurai[12] Spirit came back to life like a mythical phoenix[13]. In* this period of near starvation, fertilizers were required for food production and Chisso Company started producing Ammonium sulfate. Chisso also held monopoly over the *production of Polyvinyl chloride* (PVC), which required a thorough scientific and technical knowledge of acetylene chemistry, in the post-war period. In the 1950s, Chisso was able to increase its production of acetaldehyde and PVC. The company made use of large amounts of Mercury compounds as reaction catalysts and waste production products were discharged into the Minimata bay.

The Chisso Company started manufacturing acetaldehyde in 1932 and produced 210 tons that year. [9] By 1951, production had jumped to 6000 tons per year and in 1960, production volume peaked 45,245 tons. [12] Chisso contributed a quarter to a third of Japan's total acetaldehyde production. The chemical reaction used to produce acetaldehyde used Mercury sulfate as a catalyst. In August 1951, the co-catalyst was changed from Manganese dioxide to Ferric sulfide. [13] A byproduct of this catalytic cycle was a highly toxic organic mercury compound called methyl mercury. [14] This dangerous by-product was being released into Minimata bay from 1932 to 1968 (for thirty six years) till its production route was terminated. [15]

In post-war Japan, the city of Minimata was still dominated by feudalistic relationships, which revolved around Chisso chemical company and its manufacturing complex. [9] The economic prosperity enjoyed by the city was governed by the rise and fall of Chisso chemical company. In the day and age of democracy, such medieval relationships had serious implications in terms of public health and general environmental awareness.

---

[12] **Samurai** were the military nobility of medieval and early-modern Japan. In Japanese they are usually referred to as *bushi* [16]

[13] A **phoenix** or **phenix** is a long-lived bird that is cyclically regenerated or reborn. Associated with the sun, a phoenix obtains new life by arising from the ashes of its predecessor. [17]

II.5   DETERMINING THE CAUSE OF MINIMATA DISEASE

After the official recognition of the disease on 1st May, 1956, patients started streaming in. [3, 18] This unknown disease was called the *'strange disease'* and on May 28, the *'Minimata Strange Disease Action Committee'* was formed by the Minimata Health Center, Minimata City, the City Medical Association, the Municipal Hospital, and the Chisso Hospital. The 'strange disease' was suspected to be infectious and as a precaution patients were quarantined and their homes disinfected. Though later the disease was proven not to be contagious, the initial response contributed to the *stigmatization* and *discrimination* experienced by Minimata victims. [7] On August 24, 1956, the *Kumamoto University Study Group* was formed to investigate the cause of the disease. Researchers from the University frequently visited Minimata Bay and admitted patients to the University Hospital for regular examinations. [18]

II.5.1   THEORIES TO EXPLAIN THE CAUSE OF THE DISEASE

After extensive field surveys, clinical observations, autopsies, and testing of samples of drinking water, soil, sea water, fish and shellfish collected from the area, the Kumamoto University Study Group reported that the disease was not infectious but a kind of heavy metal poisoning. [3, 18] The *heavy metal* entered the human body through consumption of fish and shellfish found in the area. As soon as a heavy metal was identified as the cause, Chisso Company's waste water was suspected to be the source. The company's own tests revealed many heavy metals in the waste water, including *Lead, Mercury, Manganese, Arsenic, Thallium, Copper and Selenium.* It was arduous and time-consuming to determine the exact heavy metal. At first, *Manganese* was thought to be the causative agent; then *Thallium, Selenium and a multiple contaminant theory was proposed.* However, in March 1958, visiting British neurologist Douglas McAlpine suggested the cause to be *organic mercury agents*. Hence, the investigation focused on Mercury. *In February 1959, an investigation of the Mercury distribution in Minimata Bay revealed large quantities of Mercury in fish, shellfish and sludge from the bay. Pollution was heaviest around the Chisso factory wastewater canal in Hyakken harbor (see Fig. 4) and got reduced/decreased towards the sea.*

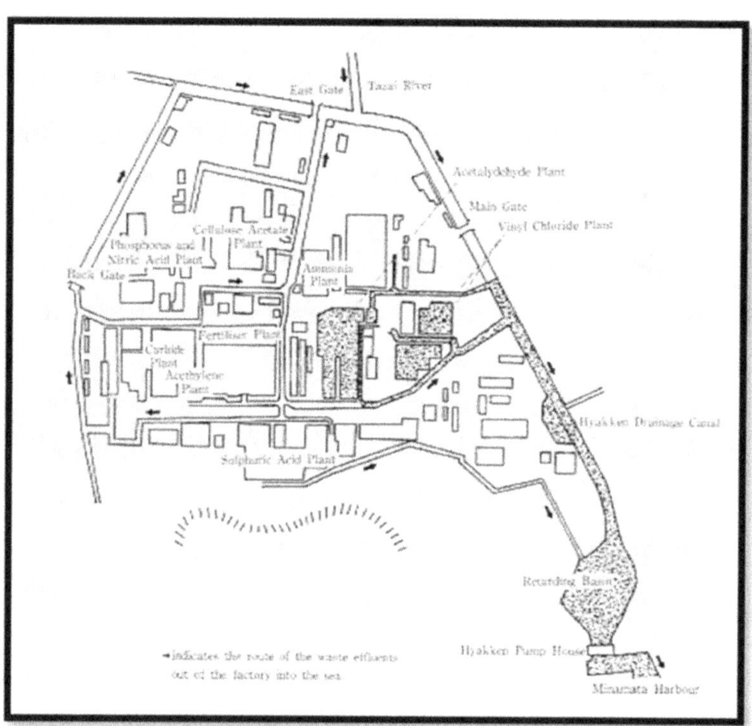

Fig. 4: Chisso's toxic effluents with methyl mercury in them was discharged into the sea, untreated, for 36 years (from 1932 to 1968). (They included other poisonous heavy metals and chemicals, such as Selenium, Thallium and Manganese.) The total amount of methyl mercury released is estimated at 400--600 tons. It is widely believed that all the mercurial sludge at the sea bottom cannot be recovered. [19]

Finally, in July 1959, based on the pathological and clinical research of Professor Tadao Takeuchi and Assistant Professor Haruhiko Tokuomi, the Kumamoto Study Research Group declared that '*Minimata disease is a disease of the Central Nervous System caused by eating fish and shellfish of the local area (Minimata bay). Mercury has come to our attention as a likely cause of pollution of the fish and shellfish.'* Such claims, however, were refuted by Kumamoto Prefectural Assembly, Chisso, who claimed that Kumamoto University's organic Mercury theory was an assumption and not based on actual proof. In the same year, Chisso Hospital conducted its own experiments in which cats were fed with factory waste water and those cats developed Minimata disease. However, these significant findings were concealed from Kumomoto Research Group. [20] Attempts were made to divert attention from Mercury, by proposing alternative theories, such as, poisoning caused by *amines*. [3]

It was not until 1960 that Professor Makio Uchida of the Kumamoto Study Research Group extracted *a crystal of an organic Mercury compound* from the shellfish of Minimata Bay. [3] In 1962, Professor Katsurou Irukayama declared that *methyl mercury chloride has been isolated* from Mercury drugs of an acetaldehyde acetic acid factory. In February 1963, The Kumamoto University Study Group concluded that the cause of Minimata disease is a methyl mercury compound found both in the shell fish and in the sludge from Chisso Company. However, structures of the two chemicals did not match.

II.5.2 OFFICIAL OPINION

The Minimata Food Poisoning Special committee of the *Ministry of Health and Welfare Food Sanitation Investigation Council* reported in 1959 that the organic mercury compound found in fish and shellfish around Minimata bay is the main causative factor of Minimata disease. [3]

However, the Japanese Government recognized Minimata disease as a pollution-related disease in September 1968 only after the second outbreak of Minimata disease in Niigata Prefecture in 1965. [3] In 1967, the Niigata Minimata disease patients sued Showa Denko as the source of contamination and took the compensation claim to Niigata District court.

II.6 ECOLOGICAL IMPACT- BIOACCUMULATION AND BIOMAGNIFICATION

Ecological consequences, although dilute and circuitous, usually form a closed loop. [2, 21] Discharged waste materials eventually find their way into human beings. In this case, organomercury waste produced from Chisso's manufacturing process was thrown in the Minimata Bay. Mercury can be traced through the waste water into organisms living in the bay, and then into cats and dogs and finally, into human beings. The Minimata disease case study is an excellent illustration of the concepts of *Bioaccumulation*[14] and *Biomagnification*[15].

Due to Mercury's bioaccumulative properties, fish and shellfish were being overexposed to methyl mercury. [3, 15, 22, 23 and 24] Mercury was then transmitted from the body tissues of the fish to organisms consuming the fish, i.e. cats, dogs and eventually human beings. Assays of tissue from dead fish and shellfish from the bay, and from cats and humans, who were exposed to poisoning, show high concentrations of Mercury. Kidney and liver concentrations show how the bodies tried to excrete the metal unsuccessfully and detoxify the body. Minimata's food chains illustrate the 'concentration of Mercury' in successive trophic levels (see Fig. 5). Table 1 depicts how Mercury concentrations progressively increased with each trophic level. *Scientists*

---

[14] **Bioaccumulation** refers to the accumulation of substances, such as pesticides, or other chemicals in an organism. Bioaccumulation occurs when an organism absorbs a toxic substance at a rate greater than that at which the substance is lost. [25]

[15] **Biomagnification**, also known as bioamplification or biological magnification, occurs when the concentration of a substance, such as DDT or Mercury, in an organism exceeds the background concentration of the substance in its diet. This increase can occur as a result of persistence – where the substance cannot be broken down by environmental processes. [26]

estimated the biomagnification of Mercury was as great as a million fold.

Mercury concentrates in the neural tissues of living organisms. Initially, the impact is loss of peripheral sensation and restriction of the visual field. In overexposed cases, patients show atrophy of the brain. The granular cells of the cerebellum are specifically targeted resulting in ataxic gait, tremors and at times violent convulsions of patients (See Section II.2).

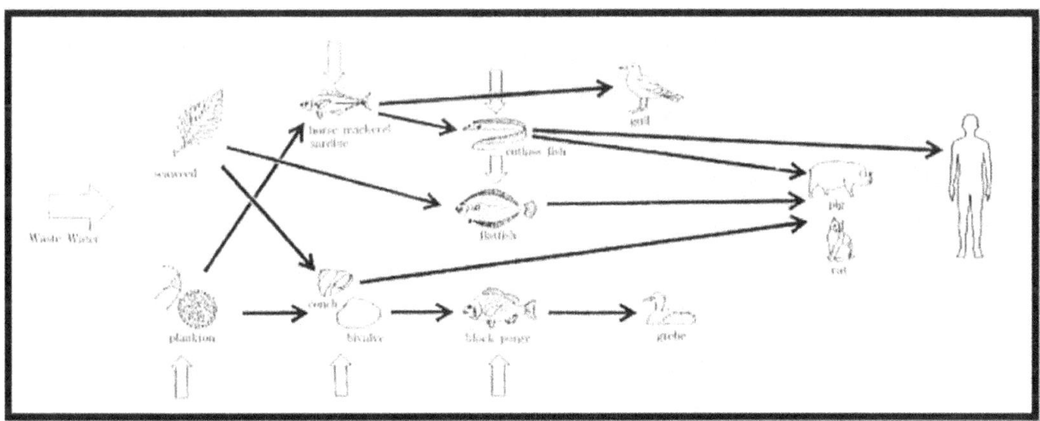

Fig. 5: Methyl mercury in the effluents, when discharged into the sea, is diluted, but it is also true that, as it travels through the food chain, it is concentrated tens or hundreds of thousand-fold and accumulates in the internal systems of marine creatures. Methyl mercury is absorbed by plankton that is eaten by fish and shellfish. It is also directly absorbed through fish's gills and skin. Some fish, like striped mullets, take their food with the mud at the seabed, and the mercury sediments in the mud go into their systems. Fish, too, got Minamata disease. Organisms higher up in the food chain, e.g., birds, cats, dogs and pigs ate these fish and became ill. Finally, man became ill. [27]

Table 1: Mercury Concentrations in Tissue Samples (ppm) [3]

Fish & Shellfish	Mercury Conc. (ppm)	Cats	Mercury Conc. (ppm)	Humans	Mercury Conc. (ppm)
Oyster	5.6	Control	0.9-3.66	Control	< 3.0
Gray mullet	10.6	Kidney	12.2-36.1	Kidney	3.1-144.0
Short-necked clam	20.0	Liver	37-145.5	Liver	0.3-70.5
China Fish	24.1	Brain	8-18	Brain	0.1-24.8
Crab	35.7	Hair	21-70	Hair	96-705

II.7 MEASURES TO CONTROL ENVIRONMENTAL POLLUTION AND CORRESPONDING LITIGATION

II.7.1 WASTEWATER TREATMENT

In 1959, Chisso as per the orders by the Ministry of International Trade and Industry installed a *cyclator purification system* and inaugurated it with a special ceremony. Kiicho Yoshioka, Chisso's President, drank a glass of water from the cyclator to demonstrate that it was safe. However, in reality the wastewater from the acetaldehyde plant was not treated by the cyclator. Testimony at a later Niigata Minimata disease trial proved that Chisso knew that the cyclator was completely futile- *'the purification tank was installed as a social solution and did nothing to remove organic mercury"*. Nevertheless the trick worked and all parties believed that factory's wastewater was safe. [18]

In August 1960, the *refined drain recycling system* was installed and was partially effective. In June 1966, effluent containing methyl mercury ceased to be discharged due to actualization of a *complete effluent processing system* and in May, 1968, the *pollution source disappeared as production of acetaldehyde was discontinued.*

In February 1969, the Economic Planning Agency established standards of water quality under the *(now former) Water Quality Law* and started regulation of methyl mercury under *(the former) Factory Effluent Law*. In December 1970, the *Water Pollution Control Law* was enacted and this was followed by nationwide uniform regulation of the discharge of toxic substances such as Mercury. [3] *Requirement for mercury level was established at 5 ppb and alkyl mercury should not be detected at all.*

II.7.2 MEASURES TAKEN TO CONTROL CONTAMINATION OF FISH AND SHELLFISH [3]

Steps taken in this direction have been summarized in Table 2.

Table 2: Measures taken to control Contamination of Fish and Shellfish

Date	Measures Implemented
1956	Kumamoto Prefecture implemented voluntary restrictions on fishing and consumption of fish and shellfish
1957	An attempt was made under Article 4 of the *Food Sanitation Act* to prohibit capturing of fish and shellfish for retail purposes from Minimata Bay. However, the Ministry of Health and Welfare refused to implement the Act resulting in the Minimata Fisheries Co-op placing self-imposed restrictions on harvest from Minimata Bay
1962	Voluntary restrictions on fishing were uplifted as a result of Chisso establishing an effluent treatment device
1964	The Co-op completely removed all restrictions on harvesting in the bay
May 1973	Kumamoto University Second Minimata Disease Medical Study Group announced that fish and shellfish of Minimata bay were still unsafe. Subsequently, the Fishing Co-op once again imposed voluntary restrictions by restricting fishing areas and organizing parole boats.
July 1973	Government enacted '*Provisional Regulatory Standards for the level of Mercury in Fish and Shellfish*' requiring total Mercury to be < 0.4ppm and alkyl Mercury < 0.3ppm
January 1974	Construction began of *dividing nets, which would close off the mouth of Minimata Bay and prevent the spread of contaminated fish. The nets closed off the bay for 23 years until their complete removal in 1997*

Table 2: Measures taken to control Contamination of Fish and Shellfish (contd.)

Date	Measures Implemented
April 1975 to March 1990	The Minimata Fisheries Co-op prohibited fishing in Minimata bay during implementation of Pollution Prevention operations
1975, 1978, 1981	In 1975, the Kumamoto Prefecture, Minimata City and Minimata Fisheries Co-op set up notice boards calling the public to exercise restraint regarding fishing; in 1978, Minimata City employed a *full time supervisor to police people* and then in 1981, the City set up an *Ocean Patrol* using fishing boats to police fishers in the bay
July 1992 to October 1997	Under the 'Agreement Relating to Compensation for the Fishing Industry', Chisso was forced by the Minimata fisheries Co-op to purchase fish and shellfish caught in the bay (until dividing nets were removed)
February 1995	Dividing nets on the outer side of the Nanatsuse zone were dismantled
1997	The Kumamoto Prefecture Governor Fukushima announced the complete removal of the dividing nets, which including anchors, sounding equipment and supplemental facilities.
15 October 1997	*Minimata Bay was re-opened as a general fishing zone and Minimata Fisheries Co-op started harvesting fish after a period of 24 years. However, as a precaution Mercury levels in fish species were tested twice a year until 2000.*
March 1958	In March 1958, the Government and Kumamoto Prefecture established the *Shallow Waters Landfill Project* (setting up of concrete blocks for fish nests and depositing of rocks to encourage sea weed growth) in areas of pollution-free sea; In 1959, the Prefecture encouraged fishing in nearby seas and culturing of mother pearls; in 1960, the Government and Kumamoto Prefecture provided financial assistance to the Minimata Fisheries Co-op to purchase fishing vessels.

II.7.3 ENVIRONMENTAL RESTORATION PROJECT [3]

Chisso factory used Mercury as a catalyst to manufacture acetaldehyde and vinyl chloride for 36 years. During this period, 70-150 tons of Mercury mixed with the effluent was discharged into Minimata Bay. Sedimentary sludge that settled on the Ocean floor contained more than 25 ppm of total Mercury with a total volume of 1.51 million m^3 and covering an area approximately 2.09 million m^3. There were areas in the depths of the bay, where the sludge was 4 m thick.

Table 3 summarizes efforts to revert the damages caused.

Table 3: Measures Taken to Restore the Environment

Date	Measures Taken
October 1977- March 1990	*Minimata Bay Pollution Prevention Project* was initiated to dispose of sedimentary sludge containing > 25ppm of Mercury. It took 13 years to complete the project and cost ¥48.5 billion (INR 26.89 billion).
1987-1988	*Marushima Port Pollution Prevention Project* was a cleaning up project to remove sedimentary sludge and restore the environment to its original state. The total expenditure for this project was ¥171 million (INR 94.82 million).
October1986- March 1988	*Marushima and Hyakken Waterway Pollution Prevention Project* was initiated to clean up 12.124m^3 of sedimentary sludge settled in the 15,000m^2 of Marushima Waterway Pool and the 1.148m length of Marushima Waterway; and 21.646m^3 of sludge settled in the 9.630m^2 of the Hyakken Waterway Pool and the 1.129m Hyakken Waterway. The total cost of the project was ¥1,554 million (INR 861.68 million).

II.8   COMPENSATION AND CORRESPONDING LITIGATION [3]

II.8.1   COMPENSATION RECEIVED BY VICTIMS

Table 4 traces compensation given to victims of Minimata disease:

Table 4: Compensation Received by Victims of Minimata Disease

Date	Measures Implemented
1956	During the initial outbreak, patients were kept in isolated wards and were exempt from medical fees and charges. In case the head of the family was affected, their families were supported by public welfare assistance and medical allowance.
1959	After the Kumamoto University Study Group's preliminary finding that Mercury is the causative agent, the Minimata Strange Disease Victims' Mutual Aid Society demanded compensation from Chisso. After much debate and deliberations, the 'Mimaikin' Solatium agreements were signed on 30th December of that year. Under this agreement, a lump sum compensation of ¥300,000 (INR 166,348) was provided for each deceased individual, an annual stipend for surviving victims (¥100,000 (INR 55,449) for adults and ¥30,000 (INR 16,634) for children), and ¥20,000 (INR 11,089) towards funeral expenses. In addition, further clauses were added, which forbade victims from making further claims. Also, if Chisso's factory effluents were shown not to be the cause of the disease, then the Solatium agreements will be dissolved immediately. Even by contemporary standards, these amounts were very little.
1964	New regulations in Kumamoto Prefecture introduced the Screening and Certification Committee for Minimata Disease Patients

Table 4: Compensation Received by Victims of Minimata Disease (contd.)

Date	Measures Implemented
1969, 1974, 1987	In December 1969, the *Law Concerning Special Measures for the Relief of Pollution-Related Health Damage* came into effect. On 27th December of that year, the Pollution-Related Health Damage Certification Council was established in Kumamoto and Kagashima Prefectures, which corresponded with a legal Certification System. In 1974, this law became the '*Pollution Related Health Damage Compensation Law*' and in 1987, it was renamed the '*Law Concerning Compensation for Pollution-Related Health Damage*'. This law continues to be the basis of certification process of victims.

By the end of August 2007, the total number of certified patients was 2,268 persons, including 1,778 in Kumamoto Prefecture and 490 in Kagoshima Prefecture. 50 years have passed since the initial occurrence of the disease and 639 patients were alive by 2007. A small number of new patients are authorized now but they are people who were afflicted by the disease in the past. [3]

II.8.2 RESPONSE OF MINIMATA CITY [3]

- Initially, Minimata city treated the disease as infectious. The Minimata City Sanitation Division scattered insecticide and disinfected areas where victims had been discovered. Patients were placed in the City Hospital's isolation ward.

- In July 1959, a special ward specifically for Minimata disease patients was completed.

- In 1965, the first public rehabilitation-specific hospital, the Minimata Municipal Hospital affiliated to Yunoko Hospital was inaugurated. However, this facility was closed in 2005 after 40 years due to its deteriorating condition and improvement of rehabilitation services at the Minimata General Hospital in Tenjin-cho, Minimata.

- In 1972, Meisuien, a social welfare institute for the severely handicapped patients was opened for Minimata disease sufferers.

- In 1969, the Yunoko Branch of Minimata Daiichi Elementary School was opened in a room of the Yunoko Hospital as an educational facility to enable serious congenital Minimata disease patients hospitalized in Yunoko Hospital to study while undergoing treatment for their handicaps. In 1975, the Yunoko Branch of Minimata Daiichi Junior High School was established at Minimata Municipal Hospital. In total 24 students comprising patients of Yunoko Hospital and patients of Meisuien graduated from there and in March, 1999, both schools were closed.

- Between 1971 and 1974, the Minimata Bay Coastal Citizens Health Survey was conducted; in 1975, a health survey of more than 7000 citizens from mountainous regions such as Kugino, Yude and Fukagawa was conducted. Until 1981, a health survey of 37,000 people was conducted.

- From 1977 to 1988, a survey of the residual Mercury levels in the umbilical cords of embryos (1,040 tested) and the hair of infants (288 tested) were conducted. In May 1990, it was declared that there was no danger of Minimata disease among infants.

II.9   SOCIAL AND POLITICAL CONSEQUENCES

II.9.1 SOCIAL CONSEQUENCES

Since the disease was related to the dancing behavior of cats, the disease became stigmatized and unfortunately, many times the stigma was self-created. In the Japanese view of medicine, the body should be in balance with nature (similar to the Ayurvedic system of medicine) and any sickness, then, is interpreted as 'deserved'. [2] Victims, therefore, were responsible for their own condition. In addition, diseased patients were ostracized by other residents.

There was discrimination of another kind fueled by general 'ignorance' (about the symptoms) and 'prejudice' (doubt whether patient is truly afflicted) about the disease. After a long struggle, Chisso agreed to pay compensation to patients in 1973. Unfortunately, compensation gave rise to a new wave of malicious slander and envy that added to patients' grief and anguish. In the early 1970s, when many new patients came forward to claim compensation, they were accused of being 'fake'.

II.9.2 POLITICAL CONSEQUENCES

In the 1950s and 60s, Chisso employed 60% of the town's workforce. [2] Chisso Company was, thus, both the *provider* and *protector* and had taken over the role of patriarchal landlord from feudal Japan. The employees were dependent on Chisso for their livelihood and in turn, honored the company with their loyalty. When fishermen began to demonstrate against Chisso, there were counter-demonstrations by the Company's employees. *To have admitted Chisso's "guilt" would have been to acknowledge that the corporation had abandoned its filial responsibility and that the relationship, now violated, could no longer be trusted.*

Given the feudal structure of Japanese society, it is therefore, not surprising that when the first few cases of Minimata disease were reported, they were suppressed, rights of victims were not recognized and no compensation was given. Instead the victims were ostracized by the society due to ignorance about the disease. [20]

Diseased victims, fishing families and company employees were excluded from debates regarding their future. Progress would only be made when victims were allowed to attend meetings to discuss the issue. Sentiments of the victims, the public and environmental protesters contributed a great deal in the *democratization process of Japan*. The media also contributed to the process of democratization by disseminating information about the Minimata disease and the pollution it caused.

II.10 EPILOGUE

Minimata City established the Minimata Disease Municipal Museum in 1993 to disseminate information about the tragedy. [3] Minimata memorial was completed in 1996, the 40th anniversary of the discovery of Minimata disease. From 1997 to 2005, the Minimata Disease Victims' Memorial Service was held annually on the memorial site. However, the story will not be complete without an excerpt from Michiko Ishimure's book, the most poignant literary description about the sufferings of the victims of Mercury pollution. [28]

'The Mother of a Weed: Sugihara Yuri'

Sugihara Sato's account of her daughter Yuri:

Sugihara Yuri, Minimata Disease Patient No. 41.

The seventeen year-old, beautiful blind girl had shown no signs of a conscious existence whatsoever since the age of six. The press called her "the milk-drinking doll". Unable to arrest her ineluctable decay, modern medicine had labeled her, in even crueler fashion, a "human vegetable."

"If Yuri is no longer a human being, but a tree or a weed, I am the mother of a tree or weed. If Yuri is a lizard, I am a lizard's mother. If she is a bird, I am a bird's mother; if she is an earthworm, I am an earthworm's mother.........."

"They say if you die a natural death, Amida Buddha will take over your soul and lead it straight to His Pure Land paradise. But who will take charge of a soul dissolved in_organic mercury? Will Chisso do it? What will the Company do with all the souls they killed? To Yuri, both this world and the other world are nothing but a deep darkness. She has no place to go when she dies her soul will never rest in peace. Even if I go to the Pure land Paradise when I die, I won't find her there. Where is Yuri's soul, dear? Where has it gone? What is its destination?"

II.11 SUMMARY

Chisso Corporation was established in Japan in 1908 as a carbide plant. In the 1930s, it began to produce chemical compounds derived from acetylene with Mercuric sulfate as a catalyst. All the waste products from manufacture of various products were dumped into Minimata Bay without treatment. This initially led to contamination of fish and then, through biomagnification, affected organisms higher up in the food chain. This chapter describes how the cause of the Minimata disease was determined; ecological impact- biomagnification and bioaccumulation; measures to control pollution and environmental laws that were implemented as a fallout; and compensation given to victims and the resultant litigation.

3 BAIA MARE

"Water is the most critical resource issue of our lifetime and our children's lifetime. The health of our waters is the principal measure of how we live on the land."

Luna Leopold, Hydrologist

III.1 INTRODUCTION

III.1.1 GEOGRAPHY

BAIA MARE is a municipality in northwestern Romania on the banks of Sasar River. [1, 2] It is the capital of Maramures County that consists of the old 'lands' of Maramures-Chioarul, Lapus, and Baia Mare Depressions. [3] The city is located at about 600 km from Bucharest, 70 km from the border with Hungary, and 50 km from the border with Ukraine as is shown in Fig.1. The city is situated in the south of Gutâi and Ignis mountain that are a part of the Eastern Carpathian mountain system as depicted in Fig.2. The area is famous for its picturesque landscapes and complex geological features such as hills, plateaus, lowlands, depressions, floodplains and terraces. The mountains also provide skiing slopes.

Baia Mare is located in a valley and is surrounded on all sides by hills and mountains, which makes the climate milder. Chestnut trees, that require Mediterranean climate to grow, can be found in the suburbs of Baia Mare as a result of this mild climate. Indeed 'the chestnut festival' is one of the symbols of this mountain town. [4] The summers are mild, cooler than the rest of the country. During winters, temperatures can abruptly drop below -20°C. Precipitation is quite high as mountains prevent air masses to pass beyond the region's limits; the average rainfall is almost 1000 mm/year. The city of Baia Mare is considered as one of the quaintest cities in Romania due to its location in the Eastern Carpathian Mountains.

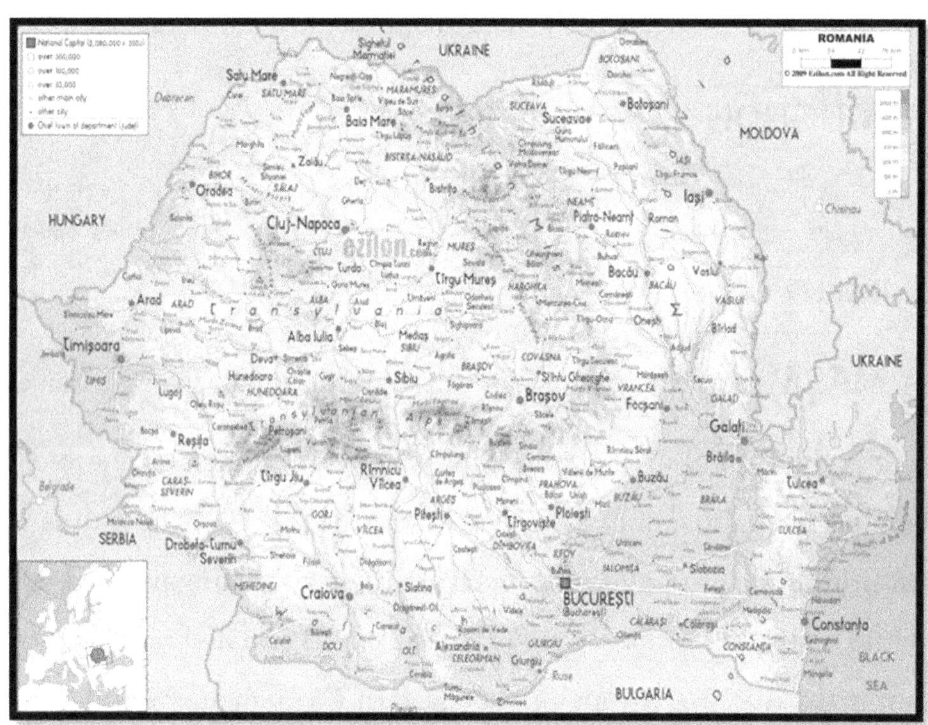

Fig. 1: Physical Map of Romania [5]

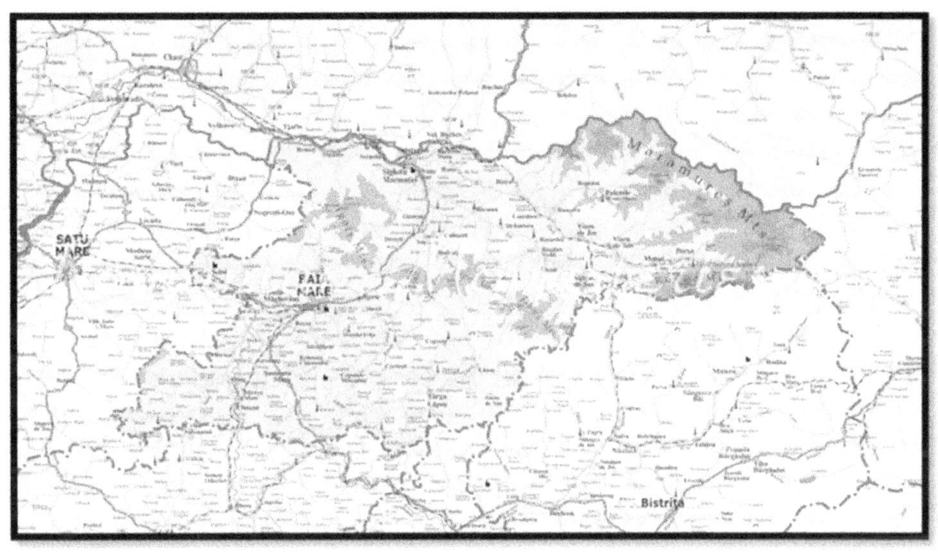

Fig. 2: Road Map of Maramures County [6]

III.1.2 ECONOMY

The primary source of livelihood for the people of Baia Mare used to be mining till the 1980s. [7] After the 1989 revolution and changes in the industrial sector, such as mining activities declined considerably. The economy and consequently, occupations got diversified. The largest sofa manufacturing plant in Eastern Europe, *Italsofa*, is located near the Baia Mare city highway ring.

III.1.3 THE COMPANY [3, 8 AND 9]

Aurul, the mine operator, is a stock company jointly owned by the Australian company Esmeralda Exploration and Remin Romania. Before beginning its operations in May 1999, Aurul obtained all environmental permits required by Romanian law for its plant in Baia Mare. According to the arrangement, Aurul would earn profits through its mining operations and Romanian authorities would benefit from Aurul's management and removal of Baia Mare's old contaminated ponds, which prevented development of the city. The company started its extraction process from an existing 30 year old tailing dam[16] (*Sasar, Meda dam*) near Baia Mare city, close to the residential area. [3] The source of raw materials for the company was mining residues from former gold and silver extraction processes, accumulated in the Meda tailing dam. Aurul's technology employed high concentrations of free cyanide in processing waters for extraction of precious metals. The whole process was designed to operate in a closed circuit with cyanide containing waters being re-used after sedimentation in the Aurul pond. Other tailing dams that were planned to be mined were *Central Flotation* (10.5 million tons with a recoverable gold grade of 0.48 gm gold per ton) and *Old Bozanta* (8.5 million tons with a recoverable gold grade of 0.30 gm gold per ton). [3]

The company claimed to have technology to clean up the by-product of gold mining from previous operations- *toxic tailings* that were being scattered as toxic dust. The company also promised to extract the remaining gold from them *via* the *gold cyanidation process*. Aurul's process and technology- Carbon-in pulp (Clearing in Place)- to be used at the Baia Mare plant was new to Romania and was supposedly modern, safe, efficient and environment-friendly. [3,9] This technology was used for recovery of gold and silver from tailings with low content of precious metals, obtained from previous processing of ores. The Baia Mare plant was designed to process 2.5 million tons of tailings per year in order to recover about 1.6 tons of gold and 9 tons of silver per year. The project was supposed to last 10 to 12 years subject to further negotiations. [3, 9]

---

[16] **Tailing dam:** A dam made from material having sufficient permeability to allow moisture to drain through over a regulated period. The dam is constructed to retain the water-sodden, fine-grained materials (tailings) that represent the waste product from a mineral-processing plant. [10]

In order to achieve both the above targets, tailings were to be transported 6.5 km away to a new dam near Bozinta Mare village, Maramures County. The process was designed to release minimal waste to the surroundings. [9] However, the company could not determine how often the plant had been inspected previously by government authorities and soon after operations began in 1999, two leaks were reported in the pipeline system. Fig. 5 describes the locations of Baia Mare and Aurul Plant and ponds. (See Section III.1.7)

III.1.4 HEAVY METALS IN BAIA MARE AND MARAMURES COUNTY

Gold is not the only heavy metal mined in the Baia Mare area. Remin, a state-owned mining company supplies rocks containing metal ores to three partly foreign-owned firms – Gold to Aurul, Copper to Allied Phoenix and Lead to Rom-Plumb. [8, 9] Maramures County is rich in Gold, Silver, Lead, Copper and salt and is historically known for mining. [3, 9] There are seven key mining sites in the County that are potential sources of pollution. They produce Gold, Silver, Lead, Zinc and Manganese. Waste waters and materials from these sites are stored in *flotation ponds* and *tailing dams*, which is standard international practice. However, the quality and protection of such dams depends on location and technology used. The Environmental Protection Agency (EPA) lists 215 dams from mining operations in Maramures County. Metallurgical plants are other potential sources of pollution. A lead smelter in Baia Mare has been used for 150 years and is reported to be heavily contaminated. Fig. 3 is a map of metallurgical and other industrial hot spots in the Tisza River Basin. Decades of such industrial activity with insufficient waste treatment has led to high levels of chronic ground water and air pollution in the County.

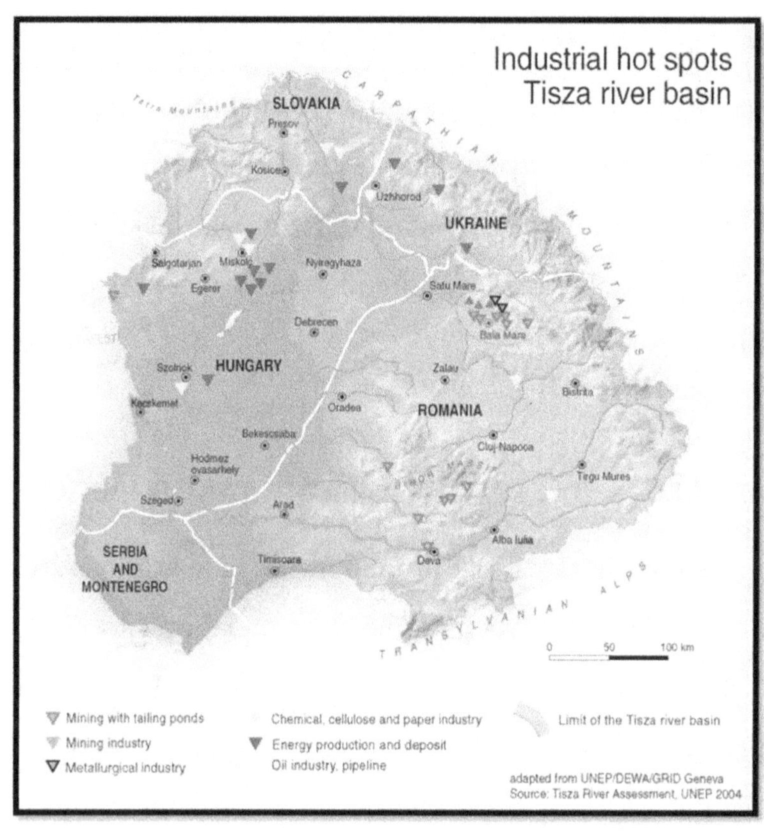

Fig. 3: Industrial hot spots in Tisza River Basin [11]

Fritz Sclingemann of the United Nations Environment Program (UNEP) noted that the cyanide spill of January 2000 contributed further to the already toxic Baia Mare region and its river systems. [12] Since the cyanide spill, heavy metals have accumulated in sediments 6-10 km downstream of Baia Mare and are likely to spread throughout the river network. [3, 13 and 14]

Heavy metals persist in the environment and bioaccumulate in living organisms. [9] This implies that the level of toxins builds up in an organism over time, hence, increasing its toxicity. Besides, toxins can also enter the food chain and biomagnify. Heavy metals pose a major threat to living organisms *via* their long-term and chronic exposure. The acute and chronic effects of Copper to humans include stomach and intestinal distress, liver and kidney damage and anemia. Copper often contained in river sediments is toxic to aquatic plants. Copper is highly soluble in water and therefore, is readily available for uptake by aquatic organisms. At low levels, lead can interfere with red blood cells chemistry, delays normal physical and mental development in babies and young children, causes slight deficits in attention span, interferes with hearing and learning abilities of children, and causes slight increases in blood pressure of adults. Chronic exposure to lead has been linked to brain and kidney disease and cancer in humans.

III.1.5 GOLD MINING OPERATION

Cyanide leach mining is now the primary method to extract gold and other metals from their respective ores by the hard rock mining industry. [15] Using cyanide for the recovery of gold was first developed in Scotland in the late 19th century. Prior to this, an inefficient *Mercury amalgamation process* was used, which recovered no more than 60% of an ore body's gold. On the contrary, leaching finely ground ore with cyanide could recover more than 97% of the ore's gold value. Cyanide *heap leaching* is a result of these early methods of processing cyanide and gold ore. In 1969, The U.S. Bureau of Mines first proposed heap leaching with cyanide as a means of extracting gold from ores that are considered too low in value to process economically. By the 1970s, the U.S. gold industry adopted the technique. Soon afterwards heap leaching became the dominant method for treating gold ores.

While the heap leaching process makes mining of even extremely low-grade ores extremely profitable, it generates a huge amount of waste. Several hundred tons of ore must be mined to produce small quantities of gold. For instance, Nevada's Carlin Trend Mine mined 129.8 million tons of ore in 1989 to recover 3.7 million ounces of gold. There are two types of leach mining- *vat and heap leaching*. In 1998, vat leaching process was used to extract about 70% of gold ores in the US and heap leaching was used to extract 30%. Overall cyanide leaching is used to process 90% of gold ores (by weight) mined in the United States.

Vat leaching is used to extract gold from ores with higher gold content (*i.e.* greater than 20 gm of gold per ton of ore), that involves holding a slurry of ore and solvent for several hours in large tanks equipped with agitators. [16] *Heap Leaching* is used for extracting gold from low-grade ores. [15,17] This process involves digging enormous pits (as big as a city), crushing the mineral ore into small chunks and heaping on an impermeable plastic or clay lined leach pad, where it can be sprayed with leach solution to dissolve the valuable metals. Operations use drip irrigation to minimize evaporation, provide uniform distribution of leach solution and minimize damage to minerals. The solution then percolates through the heap, bonding with microscopic flecks of gold and silver and leaches both the target and other minerals. The process called 'leach cycle' takes one or two months for simple oxide ores. The leach solution containing the dissolved minerals is then collected, treated in a process plant to recover the target mineral and precipitate other minerals, and then recycled to the heap after reagents levels are adjusted. Recovery can be over 90% for gold ores.

The use of cyanide in mining is becoming controversial besides being a threat to the environment. [15] Cyanide is also extremely toxic - a teaspoon of 2% cyanide solution can kill a person. Mining of low grade ores requires creation of vast open pits, unearthing and releasing dangerous toxins.

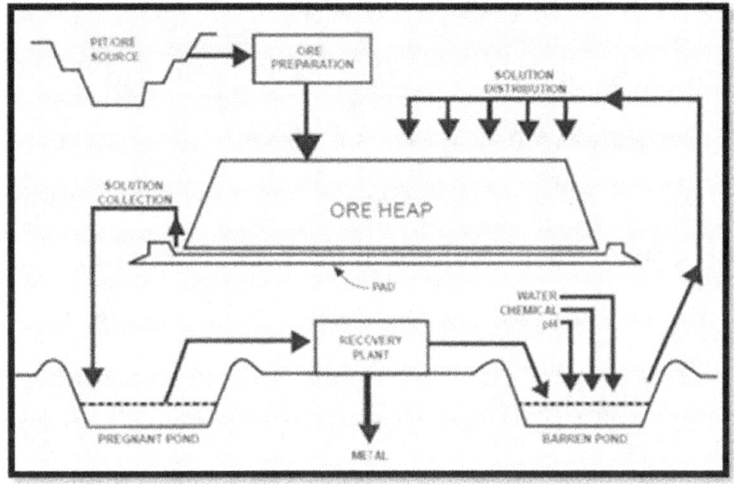

Fig.4: Schematic of typical heap leach process [18]

III.1.6 WHY ARE GOLD MINES LOCATED NEAR WATER SOURCES? [15]

Gold found in nature is in the ore form and is available only in low concentrations. From one ton of ore, only 10 gm can be excavated. Gold can be easily dissolved by cyanide. Aqueous solutions of Sodium cyanide (diluted to a concentration of 0.015-0.035% Sodium cyanide) are typically used to extract gold from its ore.

Most gold mines are located near water sources as large quantities of water are required to dilute the Sodium cyanide solutions to adequate levels of mining. Besides, having a readily available supply of water reduces transportation and other costs related to water needs.

In Baia Mare, tailings from the old Meda ponds are mixed with water to form slurry that is pumped to the nearby processing plant, where more cyanide is added as per requirement. [9] Subsequently, the slurry is pumped to the new Aurul gold mining site that is 6.5 km away.

III.1.7 AURUL PLANT AND OPERATIONS [3, 14]

The old Meda pond in Baia Mare contained 4.43 million tons of flotation solid wastes. The tailings in this pond were combined with water to form slurry. A pipeline carried the slurry to the processing plant, where cyanide was added to the mixture. High concentrations of cyanide were required in the process to extract gold and silver. After gold extraction, the tailings fluid was pumped to the new pond 6.5 km away through a pipeline.[17] To maximize gold extraction, tailings from the new dam were pumped back to the processing plant for further extraction and then again pumped to the tailing dam. Fig. 3 describes the location of various Baia Mare and Aurul plants and dams.

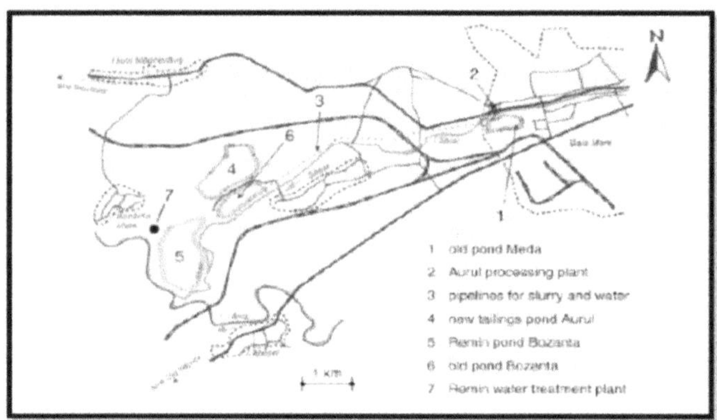

Fig. 5: Plan of Baia Mare and Aurul plant and ponds [3]

The new pond nearly 20 m high and covering 93 ha was constructed on gently

---

[17]   Cyanide concentration as derived from the Process Design Criteria for gold extraction was approximately 700 mg/L; total concentration of cyanide pumped to the new pond was approximately 400 mg/L, containing free cyanide of about 120 mg/L [17]

sloping terrain by constructing a surrounding dam and a decant well in the pond center. The decant well allowed liquid in the pond to be re-circulated to the plant. The entire pond was lined with a plastic membrane to prevent any loss to the ground. In addition, drains were fitted in the dam wall to collect any seepage, which was included in the decant well. Thus, a closed system was constructed with no loss to the surrounding environment. Groundwater pollution was monitored by installing observation wells along the perimeter. The storage capacity of the pond (between operation water level and maximum allowable water level) was found to be sufficient for extreme rain up to 118 mm.

However, there were some critical problems in the operation of the system:

a.   The old Meda pond had no liner and yet decant water with high levels of cyanide was pumped back from the new to the old pond contributing to toxic seepage

b.   Large quantities of toxic slurry and water were pumped through an extensive network of unprotected pipelines.

c.   The lining membrane of the pond was 1 mm thick under the dam and 0.5 mm thick in the pond floor area. There was no other precaution to deal with a puncture.

d.   The solids in the slurry must have sufficient coarse material to add to the dam and enough fine material to create a dry beach within the dam. Site visits on 26-27th February 2000 revealed that the dam design was faulty with respect to the quantity of coarse material.

e.   When the toxic slurry reached the new pond, tailings were separated by hydrocyclones[18] and collected on the surface of the dam, while a large quantity

---

[18]   A **hydrocyclone** (often referred to in the shortened form cyclone) is a device to classify, separate or sort particles in a liquid suspension based on the ratio of their centripetal force to fluid resistance. This ratio is high for dense (where separation by density is required) and coarse (where separation

of toxic water was stored in the pond. Hydrocyclones must be able to operate at all times for proper dam formations. However, hydrocyclone operation is difficult at low temperatures. Temperatures hit below freezing point on 21st December, 1999 and continued to stay low for five weeks. Under these conditions, hydrocyclone operation could have been paused and the tailings fluid could have been discharged directly into the pond.

f.   Except for storm run-off values, precipitation and evaporation values were missing. There was probably surplus water in the pond as the rate of evaporation is extremely uneven throughout the year and is almost non-existent in the cold months; rain water got collected at the lower end of the pond (built on inclined ground), thus, reducing the surface area for evaporation; and finally, precipitation in the Meda ponds further added to the inflow. Under these conditions, a 'closed circuit system' as per initial plans was not practical.

III.2 THE SPILL

During the winter of 1999 to 2000, the amount of precipitation in the Baia Mare area was unusually high. [3, 20] This led to accumulation of a large amount of water in the dam. However, the dam capacity only allowed accommodating storm run-off of up to 118 mm. In addition, the days before the disaster were sunny and warm resulting in melting of snow and ice and thus, further accumulation of surplus water. On 30th January 2000, there was 60-70 cm of accumulated snow in the pond and precipitation (solid and liquid) was 30 L/m^2. Besides, temperatures were above freezing point. [3]

---

by size is required) particles, and low for light and fine particles. Hydrocyclones also find application in the separation of liquids of different densities. [19]

On 30th January 2000 at 22:00, there was a break in a dam surrounding the tailings pond. [3, 9] The accident at the S.A. Aurul Company was reported by a site worker to the management. Aurul plant ceased operations and authorities were informed. The accident resulted in a spill of 100,000 m³ (3, 50,000 ft³) of cyanide-contaminated water and suspended waste (containing an estimated 50 to 100 tons of cyanide, Copper and other heavy metals). Sediments from a nearby tailing deposit were used to seal the breach, which the local authorities claim to be partially sealed by 1:30 am on 31st January 2000. Nevertheless a controlled discharge of 40-50 L/sec continued to leak from the dam that was neutralized with Sodium hypochlorite until the breach could be completely sealed.

The contaminated water spilled over into Sasar River and then into Lapus River before joining Somes River that crosses the border with Hungary at Csenger. [3, 9] Somes River is a tributary of River Tisza, Hungary's second largest river. The cyanide plume flowed from Somes into Tisza River and finally, into Federal Republic of Yugoslavia (FRY) near Tiszasziget. Travelling at 2.1-2.4 km/h, the plume took 14 days to reach FRY, which is approximately 800 km away. River Tisza is a tributary of River Danube, which flows through Serbia, Bulgaria and Rumania. The cyanide plume flowed into Danube upstream of Belgrade and continued for a further 1200 km at 2.4-2.9 km/h before entering the Black Sea. Some 2000 km of the Danube catchment area was contaminated by the spill. Fig. 6 summarizes the flow of the cyanide plume through the various river systems. [21]

The spill killed large quantities of fish in Hungary and Serbia and contaminated drinking water supplies for over 2.5 million Hungarians. [8] After the disaster, River Somes had cyanide concentrations of over 700 times of the allowed levels. [8] The spill caused interruptions to water supply of 24 municipalities and costs to several sanitation plants and industries. The amount of dead fish in Hungary was estimated to be 1,240 tones. [9] The Baia Mare cyanide spill is the biggest environmental disaster in Eastern Europe since Chernobyl.

III.3 CAUSE OF THE ACCIDENT

Several factors contributed to the spill that happened on the night of 30th January 2000. [9]

- Heavy precipitation and rapidly melting ice and snow that resulted in water rising to dangerous levels in the pond. The rise was faster than the rise of the dam that was intended to *grow gradually* as tailings accumulated. Fig. 7 explains the functioning of a tailings dam. [22]

- There was no discharge facility to deal with surplus water in the pond or to catch excess wastewater.

- The operation was open at two points- old and new ponds, which allowed unmonitored amounts of cyanide to be lost to air or ground water by evaporation or seepage/leakage respectively.

- The company and local authorities had inadequate plans given the large quantities of hazardous material being handled in the vicinity of human populations and rivers.

Fig 6: Spread of the Cyanide Spill from Baia Mare, Romania[21]

Progress of the spill plume: *1*, 30th January- Cyanide spill occurs at Baia Mare, Romania; *2*, 1 February- Spill plume reaches Romanian-Hungary border; *3*, 5 February – Cyanide registers in tests at Tiszalök; *4*, 9 February- Spill plume reaches Szolnok; *5*, 11 February – It crosses the Hungarian-Yugoslav*ia*n border; *6*, 13 February- The plume reaches Belgrade (Perlez), Yugosla*via*; *7*, 15 February- It meets the Romanian border again at Ram; *8*, 17 February- Cyanide shows up in tests at Iron Gate, Romania; *9*, 25-28 February- The plume reaches the Danube Delta.

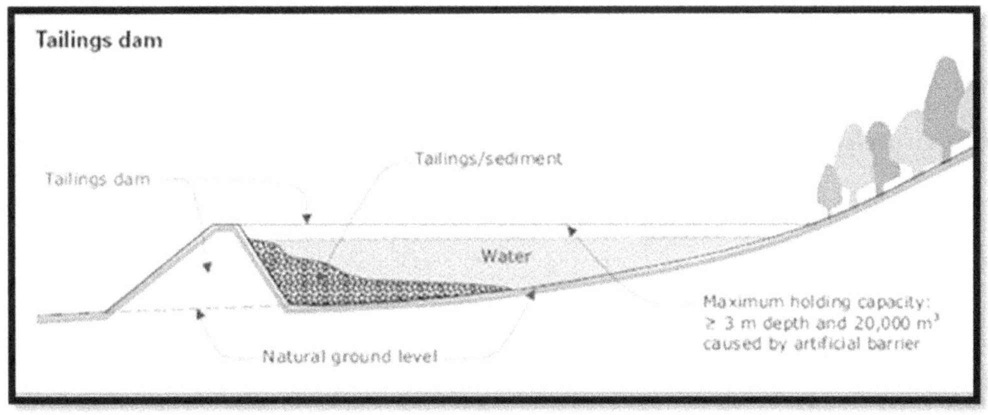

Fig. 7: How a Tailings Dam works [22]

III.4 ENVIRONMENTAL EFFECTS [3, 9 and 23]

The impact of the cyanide spill on the environment is taken from three different sources- background reports of Romania, Hungary and Federal Republic of Yugoslavia; monitoring of impacts by the three countries as the cyanide plume travelled downstream; and information collected by United Nations Education Program (UNEP)/Office for the Coordination of Human Affairs (OCHA) mission. Standard methods were used to analyze the amount of cyanides and heavy metals and the data produced by all the three countries were comparable. There were differences between the Romanian and Hungarian measurements but this could be ascribed to differences in locations and time intervals for sampling. In addition, the UN collected samples three weeks after the plume had passed and thus, could not validate any of the data produced by the three affected countries.

It also must be emphasized that certain things were handled quite methodically during the Baia Mare spill. The company was able to eventually block the flow of contaminated water from the dam. The early warning system of the International Commission for the Protection of the Danube River (ICPDR) promptly alerted downstream riparian authorities of the coming polluted waters. Towns downstream blocked pumps drawing river water and made other arrangements for drinking water. Pollution levels were also measured at critical points along the river system methodically.

III.4.1 SURFACE WATER

Overall, cyanide and heavy metal concentrations decreased rapidly with increase in distance from the spill. However, acute effects of cyanide were observed along long stretches of the river system till the intersection point of the Tisza with the Danube. Phytoplankton[19] and Zooplankton[20] communities were entirely destroyed when the cyanide plume passed. Fish were also killed when the cyanide wave passed or soon afterwards. The estimated amount of consumable dead fish found along the Tisza River in Hungary was 1240 tons. [3] However, planktons and aquatic microorganisms recovered fast due to clear water coming from upstream. Therefore, the conclusion of the study was that mud-dwelling organisms in the lower and middle Tisza regions in Hungary and Yugoslavia were not completely destroyed by the cyanide spill.

The situation in the upper Tisza (north of Tokaj, Hungary), however, was not so straightforward. Years of heavy metal mining and dam building have left these parts of the Tisza region seriously damaged and made them prone to chronic pollution. The region has several poorly maintained and operated industrial plants and ponds containing cyanide and/or heavy and agriculture.

In Romania, UN tests of the Sasar River (also known as the Dead River) showed cyanide concentrations of nearly 88 times of Romanian permissible levels. Background information showed concentrations of Arsenic and Lead in the rivers Sasar, Lapus, Somes and Tisza at 100 to 1000 times, respectively, above standard limits. Cadmium concentrations in the Sasar and Lapus rivers were also high.

In Hungary, Lead, Copper, Manganese and Iron concentrations were found to be high at certain locations along the rivers Tisza and Maros. Maros River that was not affected by the spill, showed lead concentrations four times above permissible levels.

---

[19] **Phytoplankton** are the autotrophic components of the plankton community and a key factor of oceans, seas and freshwater basin ecosystems. The name comes from the Greek words *phyton*, meaning "plant", and *planktos*, meaning "wanderer" or "drifter" [24]

[20] **Zooplankton** are heterotrophic plankton. Plankton are organisms drifting in oceans, seas, and bodies of fresh water. The word "zooplankton" is derived from the Greek *zoon*, meaning "animal", and *planktos*, meaning "wanderer" or "drifter" [24]

In the Federal Republic of Yugoslavia, Lead levels were found to be high where Tisza meets the Danube. Manganese and Iron levels were found to be high in certain parts of the Tisza and Zinc levels were high in certain parts of the Danube.

In the Danube Delta, Lead concentrations were above safety levels before and the after the passing of the cyanide plume. Cyanide concentrations were high during passing of the cyanide wave. Concentrations of other heavy metals were acceptable. Chemical hotspot locations in areas affected by the spill are summarized in Table 1.

III.4.2 SEDIMENTS

The effect of the spill on sediments was less severe in comparison to surface water. In the immediate surroundings of the broken dam, heavy metal concentration (Copper, Lead, Zinc) drastically increased. However, with increasing distance from the source, heavy metal concentration reduced. Many river systems downstream were found to have high metal concentrations in their sediments, including tributaries not affected by the spill. This included river systems in Baia Mare area and Hungary. This contamination was probably caused by previous industrial, sewage and agricultural activities conducted over a long period of time. The sediment in these areas is degraded enough to cause adverse effects on the aquatic ecosystem.

For instance, concentrations of heavy metals in the River Lapus and at the site of the spill are quite high. The concentrations for Lead, Zinc and Cadmium upstream and downstream of Baia Mare are high enough to harm mud-dwelling organisms. Zinc and Arsenic concentrations are high in the sediments of certain parts of the catchment areas of Tisza River.

Table 1: Chemical Hotspot Locations in Areas Affected by Spill [9]

Chemical	WHO Guideline 1993	EU Standard for Drinking Water	Date of Testing	Location	Concentration (μg/L)
Arsenic	10μg/L	10μg/L	1992	Baia Mare	400
Cadmium	3 μg/L	5μg/L	1992	Baia Mare/Sasar River	20
Copper	2 μg/L	2μg/L	1992	Busag/Lapus River	2200
			During spill	Cicarlau	10,500
			During spill	Romanian-Hungarian border	18,000
			UN Mission	Aurul pond	412,300
Cyanide	There are no WHO guidelines available for on acceptable standards of cyanide Hungarian standard: 100μg/L Romanian standard: 10μg/L River Rhine standard: 25μg/L		During spill	Near spill	19,400
			During spill	Satu Mare/Somes River	7,800
			During spill	Csenger	32,600
			During spill	Hun-Yug border	1,500
			UN Mission	Aurul pond	66,000-81,000
			UN Mission	Private wells, Bozanta Mare	785
			UN Mission	Danube Delta	58
Lead	10μg/L	10μg/L	1992	Cicarlau/Somes River	320
			UN Mission	Maros River	22

III.4.3 DRINKING WATER

The village of Bozanta Mare in Romania near the Aurul plant has private wells that are shallow and connected with the river. They are at a high risk of getting polluted from the Aurul pond as it is in the water catchment area of the wells. After the spill, the wells had cyanide levels nearly 80 times above permissible limits on February 10, 2000. By February 26, 2000, cyanide levels had fallen below these levels. However, the concentrations of Cadmium, Copper, Manganese and Iron were higher than permitted Romanian values. In addition, there was pollution also occurring from human and agricultural waste.

Further downstream along the River Somes, drinking water was not contaminated. However, most wells are shallow and vulnerable to surface pollution. As a result, although human health risk due to the Baia Mare cyanide spill maybe minimal but chronic health impacts due to heavy metal pollution are possible. A point to note is that there is no monitoring of water in private wells in Bozanta Mare, or groundwater monitoring downstream of Bozanta Mare, except in Satu Mare.

In Hungary, neither cyanide nor heavy metals were found in deep wells as they were well protected against surface pollution. There is probably no connection between the river Tisza and deep groundwater. Hungarian public water supply systems were also not threatened by the cyanide pollution. The surface water treatment plant in Szolnok ceased working while the cyanide plume was passing by, although treated water during the accident showed cyanide concentrations below Hungarian permissible limits. It must be mentioned here that incoming water is monitored very meticulously by the Szolnok plant for protection of its consumers.

The Becej public water supply system and two other assessed private wells were not affected by the spill in the Federal Republic of Yugoslavia.

There is probably no connection between Tisza River and deep groundwater and therefore, deep wells were not susceptible to pollution. However, these wells are not usually monitored.

III.5 SUBSEQUENT SPILLS

Five weeks after the Baia Mare cyanide spill on 10th March, 2000, a dyke burst in Baia Borsa, Maramures County and 20,000, cubic meters of Zinc, Lead and Copper-contaminated water spilt into the Tisza River. [25]

III.6 LESSONS LEARNT FROM BAIA MARE [3, 9, and 23]

The Baia Mare cyanide spill certainly was an important landmark in the history of the mining industry. Almost all parties concerned found limitations in their mandates, practices and mode of communication. Drawbacks in several functionally related issues were exposed including waste disposal technology, mine management, accident prevention, management of environment emergencies, and adequacy of current regulations to public safety and communication with the public.

Not only is public awareness about toxic chemicals, risks of mining and industrial processes low, but communication between local authorities, NGOs, and the public with respect to emergencies and disaster preparation is also poor. Communication channels need to be improved and the public should be more informed. The Awareness and Preparedness for Emergencies at the Local Level (APELL) process developed by the UNEP can serve as an important model in this regard. The local people of Baia Mare are, however, well aware of previous mining accidents, e.g., soil and groundwater have been polluted before, pipes transporting tailings have broken on several occasions, and cyanide contaminated water has been spilt outside industrial areas. The local community is also concerned about the adverse effects of mining activities on public health, particularly by cyanide and heavy metals, in Bozanta Mare and Baia Mare.

At Aurul, a complete risk assessment of operations- remining old tailings- should be carried out. In this respect, important points to be included are – whether and how hydro monitoring of the material to be remined using cyanide-containing effluent can be replaced by an environmentally less risky process; whether the materials in the plant can be processed with less toxic materials; and how improved redesigned systems, especially with regards to safety, can be put in place. Given several accidents with tailing dams, construction concepts and operation procedures need to be thoroughly reviewed. An inventory and risk assessment study should be made of all mining and related industries in the Maramures region, including abandoned sites. This will give a firm foundation for improved accident prevention, emergency preparedness and response measures.

More comprehensive and detailed sampling and analytical studies are required. For instance, analysis of composition of sediments in the new pond at Aurul to determine the amount and types of cyanide present; monitoring of water quality in the wells; multinational monitoring of long-term ecological effects of the cyanide spill on birds, mammals, and vegetation; further analysis of the chemistry and toxic effects of cyanide, especially, formation and stability of heavy metal cyanide complexes in the aquatic system; analysis of the heavy metals in sediments; agreement by all countries in the Tisza catchment area on a common set of indicators for water and sediment quality monitoring; and intercalibration study of chemical analyses of water and sediment samples among all the countries affected.

Several improvements need to be made with regards to drinking water in the three affected countries- Romania, Hungary and Yugoslavia. An inventory of current private wells and an inventory of polluted areas that endanger groundwater, surface and drinking water (entire river basin) should be created. New monitoring systems for groundwater and private wells need to be put in place. Finally, drinking water supply systems in Marmures County for private households should be changed to public collective systems.

There is an urgent requirement for broad, longer term environmental management plan and sustainable development strategy for both the Maramures region in Romania and the catchment area of Tisza River. This should address not only mining and related industries but also other economic activities such as, tourism, fishing, agriculture, biodiversity requisites and other social issues.

Finally, the UN mission failed to address the important question of 'liability and compensation' with respect to the spill and its effects. An international system can address this issue more easily. A protocol should be developed for liability and compensation on accidents with transboundary effects with the assistance of UN/ECE Convention on the Protection and Use of Transboundary Watercourses and International Lakes and the UN/ECE Convention on the Transboundary Effects of Industrial Accidents.

III.7 SUMMARY

On 30th January, 2000 at 22:00, a dam surrounding the tailings pond in Baia Mare, Romania broke. The site was a part of S.A. Aurul Company, a joint company having collaboration between the Australian company Esmeralda Exploration and the Romanian government. The accident resulted in a spill of 100,000 cubic meters of cyanide-contaminated water and suspended waste containing 50 to 100 tons of cyanide, Copper and other heavy metals. The cyanide infected water spilled over into Sasar River, then into Lapus River, before joining the Somes River that crosses the border with Hungary. The cyanide plume flowed from the Somes into the Tisza River and finally, into the Federal Republic of Yugoslavia. From the Tisza River, the cyanide plume flowed into the River Danube upstream of Belgrade and continued for a further 1200 km before entering the Black Sea. The spill killed large quantities of fish in Hungary and Serbia. Water supply to 24 municipalities was affected and several sanitation plants and industries were affected. The Baia Mare cyanide spill is the biggest environmental disaster in Eastern Europe since Chernobyl.

The description of the event is preceded by a discussion on the long history of mining of heavy metals in Marmures County and how it affects the environment and human health; how the modern process of Gold mining has evolved and that modern processes require huge amounts of cyanide; why Gold mines are typically located near water sources; and finally, how the Aurul plant operates and critical problems in its functioning.

The cause of the accident; environmental impact on surface water, sediments and drinking water; subsequent spills; and lessons learnt from the Baia Mare spill have also been elaborated.

4 LOVE CANAL

"The greatest shortcoming of the human race is our inability to understand the exponential function."

Albert A. Bartlett

"We need to defend the interests of those whom we've never met and never will."

Jeffrey D. Sachs

IV.1 INTRODUCTION

IV.1.1. GEOGRAPHY

LOVE CANAL (43° 4'50.00"N, 78°57'7.00"W) is a locality in the LaSalle section of Niagara Falls City in New York State, four miles south of Niagara Falls. [1, 2 and 3] It covers thirty six blocks (fifteen acres) along 99th Street and Read Avenue and is situated in the far southeastern corner of the city. It is home to about 800 single working class families. Love Canal is bound by two water bodies- Bergholtz Creek to the north and Niagara River one quarter mile (400m) to the south. Fig.1 is a map of the City of Niagara Falls with the Love Canal site highlighted.

IV.1.2 TOPOGRAPHY

Love Canal is located in the *floodplains* of the Niagara River and is generally flat. [4] It is dominated by three major topographical features – the United States and

Canada Falls, the Niagara gorge and the Niagara Escarpment[21].

IV.1.3 DRAINAGE

The Love Canal area is characterized by poor natural drainage due to relatively flat topography, presence of subsoils of low permeability and shallow depth of streams and rivers. [4, 6]

Streams in the Love Canal area eventually flow into the Niagara River. In the North, Bergholtz Creek and Black Creek join and flow in an east to west direction. Cayuga Creek flows in a North to South direction and flows into the Little Niagara River near South 87th Street. Little Niagara River unites with Niagara River on the west side of Cayuga Island. Due to certain climate and weather-related conditions and the gentle slopes of the three creek beds, temporary reversal of water flow directions is known to occur in Bergholtz, Black and Cayuga creeks.

Prior to the early 1970s, several surface soil features known as *swales* existed in the Love Canal area. Swales were shallow depressions less than 10 feet deep and they helped to drain the surface water runoff. Swales, probably, contributed to the migration of contaminants from Love Canal to the adjacent residential areas.

---

[21] Niagara Escarpment is a steep cliff that runs in an easterly direction from the Niagara River immediately south of Lewiston New York to well beyond the Love Canal area. [5] At the Niagara River, the escarpment is approximately 200 feet high and reduces gradually towards the east into a gently sloping incline. North of the escarpment, the land slopes gently towards Lake Ontario and south of the escarpment, the land slopes gently towards the upper Niagara River.

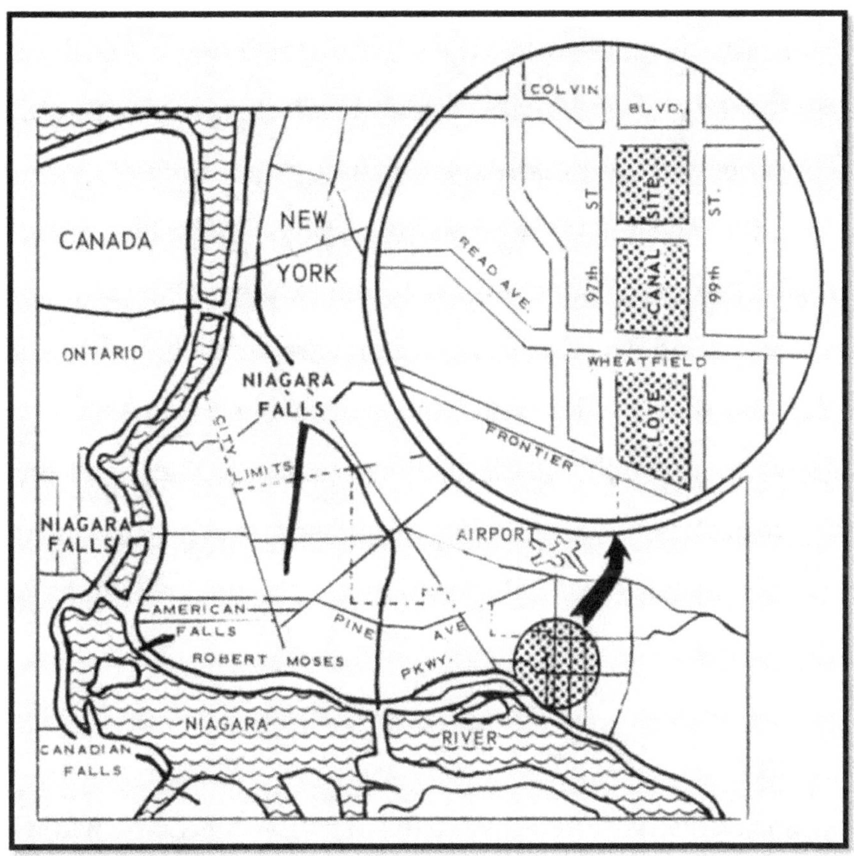

Fig. 1: Map of Niagara Falls, N.Y. highlighting the Love Canal site [7]

IV.1.4 BEDROCK AND GROUNDWATER [4]

Bedrock in the Love Canal area consists of a unit known as *Lockport Dolomite* that primarily is composed of the mineral Calcium Magnesium carbonate. It also contains secondary deposits of sulfates (gypsum) and sulfides. Beneath the Lockport Dolomite is a relatively impermeable layer, *Rochester shale. Lockport dolomite is dark grey to brown in color and is the principal aquifer in Niagara Falls. Artesian and unconfined water tables are found here. There is a vertical joint system hydraulically connected to the Niagara River.*

Lockport dolomite is covered by a layer of *glacial till,* which is reddish brown in color and consists of silty to sandy clay with gravel and cobbles. This layer was deposited by the advance and retreat of glaciers. Permeability is low in this layer. Layers of loamy to sandy clay are found throughout the Love Canal locality with varying thickness above the glacial till. This layer is called *Lacustrine deposit* and was formed in the area by lakes that were formed by melting and retreat of glaciers during the late Quaternary period. The two lakes primarily responsible for these deposits were Lake Dana and Lake Tonawanda. Deposits due to the two lakes can be distinguished by their texture and color. Deposits due to Lake Dana are reddish brown, sticky, silty clay to clay, while deposits due to Lake Tonawanda are coarser, reddish brown to gray, silty clay to clay. General permeability of this layer is again low. The lacustrine deposits are covered by silty sand, clayey silt and other *fill* materials (construction rubble and industrial waste) varying in thickness. Permeability of this layer is greater than the underlying clays.

IV.1.5 EARLY HISTORY

The Love Canal is derived from the last name of William T. Love, who visualized a canal connecting the Niagara River and Lake Ontario. [1, 8 and 9] The purpose of the canal would be to provide hydroelectricity to the area's growing industries. However, the power scheme failed due to a variety of reasons: limitations of direct current (DC) power transmission, introduction of alternating current (AC) and Congress passing a law preventing the removal of water from the Niagara River in order to preserve the Niagara Falls. [10] Besides, investors dropped sponsorship of the project due to the Panic of 1893. [11] After 1892, Love decided to build a shipping lane that would bypass the Niagara Falls, reaching Lake Ontario. He planned a community of parks and homes along Lake Ontario that he would call 'Model City'. However, his plan was never realized. Only one mile (1.6 km) of the canal, about 50 feet (15m) wide and 10 to 40 feet (3m to 12m) deep was dug and a few streets and homes were built when his funds depleted. [12]

The abandoned canal soon filled up with water. [12] In the 1920s, the canal became a dumpsite for the City of Niagara Falls' *municipal refuse*. In 1942, Hooker Electrochemical Company founded by Elon Hooker was granted permission by the Niagara Power and Development Company to dump the large quantity of chemical waste it was producing in the canal. *The canal was drained and lined with thick clay.* Hooker began depositing 55 US gal (210 L) metal or fiber barrels in the canal. In addition, the City of Niagara Falls and the US army also dumped refuse in the Love Canal during the 1940s. In 1947, Hooker bought the canal and its 70 ft (21 m) wide embankments on both sides of the canal.[10] In 1948, after World War II had ended and the City of Niagara Falls had terminated self-sufficient disposal of refuse, Hooker became the sole owner and user of this site. During the 1940s, 21,000 tons of chemicals (including twelve known carcinogens, e.g., halogenated organics, chlorobenzenes and dioxin [2]) such as "caustics, alkalis, fatty acids and chlorinated hydrocarbons from the manufacturing of dyes, perfumes, solvents for rubber and synthetic resins" were deposited in the abandoned canal. [13] The exact list of various classes of chemicals disposed in the Love Canal between 1942 and 1954 are miscellaneous acid chlorides (including acetyl, caprylyl, butyryl, nitrobenzoyl); thionyl chloride and miscellaneous sulfur/chlorine compounds; miscellaneous chlorinated products (including waxes, oils, napthenes, aniline); Dodecyl (lauryl, lorol) mercaptan, chlorides and miscellaneous organic Sulphur compounds; trichlorophenol; benzoyl chlorides and benzotrichlorides; metal chlorides; liquid disulfides and chlorobenzene; hexachlorocyclohexane; chlorobenzenes; benzyl chlorides; and Sodium sulfide/sulfhydrates. [6]

The chemicals were buried at a depth of twenty to twenty-five feet beneath the ground. [10] This *landfill* site was in operation till 1953, after that it was covered with soil and vegetation growth concealing the hazardous site.

IV.2 EVENTS THAT LED TO THE LOVE CANAL DISASTER

Soon afterwards in 1953, Hooker sold the Love Canal site to the City of Niagara Falls Board of Education, New York for $1. [2,14]   In addition, Hooker Chemical ensured that the School Board had been forewarned about the hazardous site by writing into the deed that the School Board would sign, a disclaimer of responsibility for any damages due to the buried chemicals. This would also absolve them from any future repercussions.

In January 1954, construction of the 99th Street School began and upon completion in 1955, 400 children started attending the school. [10, 13] Several other schools also opened in the vicinity to accommodate students. In 1955, a second school, the 93rd Street School opened six blocks away.

The remaining land was sold off by the school authorities for homes to be built by private developers and the Niagara Falls Housing Authority. The City of Niagara Falls also constructed sewers for a mixture of low income and single family residences in the area adjacent to the landfill site. [15, 16] The land where private homes were being built was not part of the agreement between the School and the Board and as a result, residents were not aware of the potential hazard. [10]

The clay lining of the landfill was severely tampered with. [17] The local government removed part of the clay cap to be used as 'fill dirt' for the nearby 93rd Street School and punched holes in the solid clay walls to build water lines and the LaSalle Expressway. Moreover, construction crews broke through the clay seal while building gravel sewer beds, breaching the canal walls. [18] Besides, the supposedly impermeable clay cover began to crack. [10]

There was no monitoring or evaluation of the chemical wastes that were being stored underground. [10] *With the removal of the clay cap, toxic wastes were allowed to escape when rainwater (no longer restricted by the partially absent clay cap) washed them through the gaps formed in the walls. Buried chemicals, thus, migrated and permeated from the canal. [11, 18] The construction of the LaSalle Expressway restricted groundwater from flowing into the Niagara River.* The breached canal thus became an overflowing pool following the exceptionally wet winter and spring of 1962. There were reports of puddles of oil or colored liquid in yards or basements.

IV.3 HOW THE DISASTER WAS DISCOVERED AND PUBLICIZED

The unusually high rainfall and snowfall of 1975 and 1976 resulted in high groundwater levels in the Love Canal area. [1] In certain areas, the landfill cover was washed away revealing 55-gallon drums. Surface water bodies became contaminated, basements began to ooze an oily residue and the area was filled with noxious chemical odors. Sump pumps[22] were chemically corroded and basement cinderblock walls were infiltrated. It was only in the latter half of 1976 that two reporters working for the *Niagara Gazette,* David Pollack and David Russell, reported that materials from a chemical landfill between 97th and 99th streets have been seeping into basements of homes in the area. [14] Toxic chemicals were being carried through city storm sewers and improperly discharged into the Niagara River. Chemical analyses of residues near the old Love Canal dumpsite and several sump pumps revealed 15 organic chemicals, including three toxic chlorinated hydrocarbons. The matter went quiet for a year until September 1977 when US representative John J. LaFalce and the Federal Environment Protection Agency (US EPA) began looking into the issue. [14]

Michael Brown, a journalist for the Niagara Gazette, studied in detail the Love

---

[22] A **sump** (American English and some parts of Canada: oil pan) is a low space that collects any often-undesirable liquids such as water or chemicals. A sump can also be an infiltration basin used to manage surface runoff water and recharge underground aquifers. One common example of a sump is the lowest point in a basement, into which flows water that seeps in from outside. If this is a regular problem, a **sump pump** that moves the water outside of the house may be used. [22]

Canal disaster in his book *Laying Waste*. [19] He is also noteworthy for bringing many other toxic waste catastrophes in the United States to public knowledge. As a result of various studies conducted by *The Niagara Gazette and US EPA*, New York State Health Commissioner, Robert Whalen, in August 1978, declared Love Canal to be in a state of emergency, ordered closing of 99th Street School and evacuation of pregnant women and children under the age of two from Tiers 1 and 2 of the Emergency Declaration Area (see Fig. 2) [14]. In addition, US President Jimmy Carter approved emergency financial aid for the area to relocate homes of 236 families at the cost of $10 million. [11, 14] *This was the first time in US history that emergency funds were used for a situation other than a natural disaster. [20]*

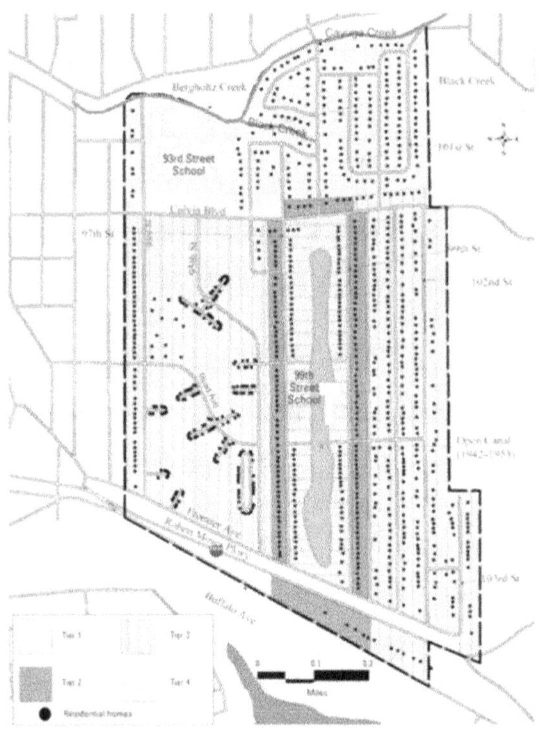

Fig. 2: Love Canal Emergency Declaration Area (EDA). [21]

IV.4 IMPACT ON THE ENVIRONMENT [4]

The hydrogeologic studies conducted by the United States Environment Protection Agency demonstrated that *there is little potential for migration of contaminants from Love Canal into the Declaration Area.* These findings are consistent with the multimedia environmental monitoring program. Besides, it was also found that the glacial till under the former canal was not breached due to excavation or dumping activities.

There was no significant general pattern of *shallow system ground water contamination* attributable directly to migration from Love Canal found outside of Tier 1 in the Canal Area. There were only some isolated pockets of shallow system ground water contamination located in areas adjacent to the former canal. Small amount of contamination was observed throughout the bedrock aquifer. *However, ground water samples from the bedrock aquifer located in the Lockport Dolomite did not reveal any pattern of contamination that had migrated directly from Love Canal.*

Soil samples collected in the Declaration Area also did not show any Love Canal related patterns of contamination. Such patterns were only seen in Tier 1 of the Canal area and were typically, associated with known or supposed transport pathways in the soil and with shallow system ground water contamination. In addition, there was no evidence of Love Canal related contamination that had migrated through former swales into the Declaration Area nor were wet area residences found to have higher concentration of contamination than dry residences.

Sump water was highly contaminated and also showed the presence of high concentrations of sorbed phase of certain organic contaminants present in the sump sediment. *The storm sewer monitoring program showed very clearly direct Love Canal related contamination in all storm sewer lines that are connected to storm sewers originating on 97th and 99th Streets. They also contributed to the distant transport of contaminants from Love*

Canal. Finally, creeks and rivers in the proximity of Love Canal related storm sewer outlets and downstream were contaminated by direct migration of contaminants from the canal through the sewer system.

Studies were also conducted for air, food and radioactive contamination, which revealed that the environmental quality of the Declaration Area was not significantly different from control sites or concentrations typically found in urban areas in the rest of the United States for which monitoring data are available.

Finally, environment monitoring studies for 2,3,7, and 8-TCDD (Tetrachloro dibenzo-*p*-dioxin) was especially carried out. This was because of the high toxicity of the 2,3,7, and 8-TCDD isomer[23] and concern among residents about potential exposure to this compound. No TCDD was detected in air samples. However, it was found in untreated leachate in the sumps of certain Tier 1 residences, sediment of storm sewers near the canal and in the sediments of local creeks and the Niagara River near outfalls of storm sewers originating from the Love Canal.

The hydrogeologic program came to the same conclusion as the multimedia environmental monitoring program that there was little potential for migration of contaminants from Love Canal into the Declaration Area. The hydrogeologic investigation also concluded that the barrier drain system that was installed around the perimeter of Love Canal in 1978 and 1979 is functioning as designed. The outward migration of contaminants through the more permeable overloaded soil has been contained. In addition, movement of shallow system ground water was towards the drain. In general, no environmental contamination that was directly attributable to the migration of contaminants from Love Canal was found in the Declaration Area with the

---

[23] TCDD regulates the expression of a wide range of drug-metabolizing enzymes, thereby, impacting several biological processes. The most well-known symptoms of severe acute intoxication are chloracne, porphyria, transient hepatotoxicity, and peripheral and central neurotoxicity. Due to the long-term persistence of TCDD in the human body, atherosclerosis, hypertension, diabetes, vascular ocular changes, and signs of neural system damage, including neuropsychological impairment, can be present for several decades after massive exposure. [22]

exception of storm sewer lines and creeks.

IV.5 IMPACT ON HUMAN HEALTH

Residents of Love Canal complained of strange odors and 'substances' surfacing in their yards. [1] Basements were covered with a thick, black substance and vegetation was dying. In many yards, the only vegetation that grew was shrubby grass. There were numerous reports of birth defects; many anomalies, for instance, enlarged feet, heads, hands and legs; abnormal incidence of miscarriages; high rate of unexplained illnesses and mental retardation; and the discovery of toxic substances in the milk of nursing mothers. [23, 24] Industrial workers were stricken by nervous disorders and cancer. Environment Protection Agency reported high white blood cell counts in blood tests, a precursor to Leukemia [20], and chromosomal damage [11] among Love Canal residents. 33% of residents had undergone chromosomal damage as opposed to 1% in a typical population. Exposed children were found with an excess of seizures, learning problems, hyperactivity, eye irritation, slum rashes, abdominal pain, incontinence and stunted growth. [23]

IV.6 SITE CLEAN-UP

In August 1978, the 99th Street School, which was located within the former boundary of the Hooker landfill site, was shut down and demolished. [1] However, neither the school board nor the chemical company accepted liability. The 93rd School Street was closed by the City of Niagara Falls Board of Education in August 1979 after further studies of chemical contaminants were released. [1]

In 1979, the Albert Elia Building Co., Inc., renamed Sevenson Environmental Services, Inc., was made the principal contractor to safely re-bury the toxic waste at the former landfill site. [25] The most toxic area (16 acres, 65000 m^2) was covered with thick plastic liner, clay and dirt. A 2.4 m (7ft 10 in) high barbed wire fence was installed around the area. [26] *Other remedial measures included installation of a leachate collection system; installation of leachate collection system components, including manholes, pump chambers; 30,000 gal holding tank; installation of 30 French drains into the landfill wastes to promote dewatering of the site; construction of an impermeable clay cap; construction and maintenance of contaminant migration and decontamination facilities; collection, handling and treatment of 3,000,000 gal of heavily contaminated groundwater; and construction and revision of storm and sanitary sewers adjacent to the Love Canal site.* [25] Cleanup of the Love Canal site was not completed until 2004 and was funded by Superfund[24]. [27]

Less than 90 of the 900 families opted to remain in the Love Canal locality subject to their homes being in an environmentally safe area. [10] In 1980, the Love Canal Area Revitalization Agency (LCARA) was established to restore the locality. The area north of Love Canal came to be known as the Black Creek Village.

IV.7 COMPENSATION/LITIGATION

In August 1978, President Carter approved emergency financial aid for the Love Canal area so New York State can start buying homes of 236 families in Tiers 1 and 2, who were relocated at a cost of $10 million. [11, 14] In May 1980, President Carter declared Love Canal a national emergency that cleared the way for relocation of 710 other families. [14]

Love Canal along with severely polluted sites, for instance, Times Beach, Missouri and Valley of Drums, Kentucky triggered the United States Congress to pass the Comprehensive Environmental Response, Compensation, and Liability Act

---

[24] **Superfund** or **Comprehensive Environmental Response, Compensation, and Liability Act** of 1980 (**CERCLA**) is a United States federal law designed to clean up sites contaminated with hazardous substances as well as broadly defined "pollutants or contaminants"[28]

(CERCLA) or the Superfund Act in 1980. [10]

The Superfund Act contained a 'retroactive liability' provision, due to which Hooker (now renamed Occidental) was held responsible for clean-up of the former landfill site even though it had followed all U.S. laws while disposing of it. [29] In 1994, the Federal District Court found Occidental *negligent but not reckless* in its handling of the waste and sale of the land to the Niagara Falls School Board. In 1995, Occidental Chemical was sued by EPA and agreed to pay $129 million as compensation. [30]

A lesser known outcome of the Love Canal disaster was the foundation of an 'environmental justice' movement. This movement emphasized the impact of toxic pollution on working class and minority communities. [2]

IV.8 SUMMARY

The story of Love Canal started with William T. Love, who at the end of the 19th century, envisioned a canal connecting Niagara River and Lake Ontario. The purpose of the canal was to generate hydroelectricity to the area's rapidly growing industries. However, his vision was never realized. Only one mile of the canal was dug, when his funds depleted and the canal was abandoned. In the 1920s, the canal became a dumpsite for the city's municipal refuse. In 1942, Hooker Electrochemical Company was granted permission by the Niagara Power and Development Company to dump its chemical waste in the canal. Additionally, the City of Niagara Falls and the US army also dumped refuse in the Love Canal during the 1940s. The landfill site was in operation till 1953, subsequently, it was covered with soil and vegetation. Soon afterwards, Hooker sold the Love Canal site to the Niagara Falls Board of Education, New York for $1 and in the deed included a disclaimer of responsibility for any damages due to the buried chemicals.

The chapter then describes the sequence of events that led to the discovery of the forgotten landfill site upon which schools and homes had been built; the impact on the environment; impact on human health; how the site was cleaned up; compensation received by victims and litigation that resulted from the incident.

5 MUMBAI OIL SPILL 2010

"Let us save what remains: not by vaults and locks which fence them from the public eye and use in consigning them to the waste of time, but by such a multiplication of copies, as shall place them beyond the reach of accident."

Thomas Jefferson

V.1 INTRODUCTION

V.1.1 GEOGRAPHY OF INDIAN COASTAL REGIONS

THE LENGTH of the mainland Indian shoreline is approximately 5700 kms and after including the two groups of islands- Andaman and Nicobar and Lakshadweep- it is about 7500 kms. [1] The western coastline includes the coastal regions of Gujarat, Maharashtra, Karnataka, and Kerala. It has a wide continental shelf with an area of roughly 0.31 million km^2 and is marked by backwaters and mud flats[25]. The eastern coast includes the coastal regions of Tamil Nadu, Andhra Pradesh, Orissa and West Bengal (Fig. 1). It covers an area of 1430 km^2 and is dominated by flat and deltaic topography rich in mangrove forests.

Mangroves are located all along the estuarine areas, deltas, tidal creeks, mud flats, salt marshes and occupy an area of about 6740 km^2 (~7% of world's mangrove forests). Coral reefs are abundant on small islands in Gulf of Kutch, Gulf of Mannar in Tamil Nadu and on Lakshadweep and Andaman and Nicobar group of islands. [2] Ecosystems consisting of coral reefs, mangroves, estuaries, deltas are rich in

---

[25] **Mudflats** or **mud flats**, also known as **tidal flats**, are coastal wetlands that form when mud is deposited by tides or rivers. They are found in sheltered areas such as bays, bayous, lagoons, and estuaries. [3]

biodiversity, protect the coastal zones from soil erosion and are also fertile grounds for fishery production. India ranked 5th in all over Asia in 1996 in fishery production.

V.1.2 OIL EXPLORATION [5]

The history of oil and gas exploration in India began in 1867 with the discovery of oil deposits in Makum, Assam. Since then several oil companies have taken birth in India. Till Independence, Assam was the only state in India where mineral oil was drilled and refined in the refinery of Digboi. This is the only oilfield in the world which has been exploited continuously for more than 100 years. After Independence, Gujarat plains and Cambay off-shore were found to have potential hydrocarbon deposits. However, major reserves were accidentally discovered off the coast of Mumbai, 115 km from the shore. This is the richest oilfield discovered till date in India and is also called the 'Bombay High'. Deposits of oil were found deep under seabed and the first offshore mobile drilling platform, Sagar Samrat, was bought from Japan to extract oil from deep coastal waters. The most recent oilfields have been discovered from offshore areas off the deltaic coasts of Godavari, Krishna, Kaveri and Mahanadi.

Gas reserves are generally associated with oilfields. Gas reserves are found in almost all the offshore oilfields of Gujarat, Maharashtra, Tamil Nadu, Andhra Pradesh, and Orissa. Exclusive natural gas reserves have been found in Tripura and Rajasthan.

V.1.3 OIL AND GAS RESERVES IN INDIA

As of January 2010, India had approximately 5.6 billion barrels of oil reserves and approximately 38 trillion ft^3 of natural gas reserves, the second largest amount in the Asia-Pacific region after China. [6] India has thirty-five major fields onshore (primarily in Assam and Gujarat) and four major offshore oil fields (near Bombay, south of Pondicherry, and in the Palk Strait). In 2009, India produced approximately 880 thousand barrels per day of total oil from over 3,600 operating oil wells. Out of this, approximately 680 thousand barrels per day was crude oil and the rest were other liquids or refinery by-products.

Fig.1: Map of India showing the States and Capital [4]

V.1.4 OIL SPILL INCIDENTS IN INDIA [5]

There has been a history of oil spills along the Indian coast as summarized in Table 1 (see Appendix A). [7] Oil spills can take place due to a number of factors. They may happen during transportation of oil. Oil is commonly transported by barges, tankers, pipelines, and trucks, each of which can lead to oil accidents. Pipelines transporting oil can develop leaks or cracks through which oil can seep into the environment. Some oil can leak while transporting from one vehicle to the other, a process called *lightering*. Weather conditions such as, hurricanes and storms, can cause tankers or barges to wreck or damage offshore drilling facilities, both of which can cause oil spills.

Oil spills can also occur during various phases of production, for example, when oil is being extracted from an oil well or being converted into other products at a refinery. Accidents can be caused by human mistakes or by machine failures. Sometimes, spilling of oil is used as a weapon of war. Illegal dumping of oil can also harm the environment.

V.2 THE EVENT

The Mumbai Oil Spill happened as a result of collision between two Panamian ships- *MSC Chitra* (IMO: 7814838) and MV *Khalija 3* (IMO:8128690)- off the coast of Mumbai on Saturday, 7 August 2010 at around 9:50 a.m. local time. [7,8] *MSC Chitra* carrying about 1200 containers was outbound from South Mumbai's Jawaharlal Nehru Port and MV *Khalija 3* was inbound heading towards Mumbai Port as shown in Fig. 2. The accident led to grounding of MV Chitra near Prongs Reef Light[26], also called Colaba

---

[26] **Prong's Lighthouse** is a lighthouse situated at the southernmost point of Bombay (Mumbai), India in the Colaba area. It was built in 1875 by Thomas Ormiston at the cost of INR 600,000. [10] Its beam can be seen from a distance of 30 kilometres. It is one of three lighthouses of the city. The lighthouse had a cannon during British rule to secure the bay. It is only accessible during low tide by the Indian Navy.

Point Light. The precise geographical position of the collision was 18°51′51.8″ N and 072°49′12.0″E.

MSC Chitra was loaded with 2,600 tons of oil and 31 containers of pesticides like pyrethrins and organophosphates at the time of the accident. The impact of the collision was so severe that the two fuel tanks on the port side of MV Chitra were ruptured, the ship tilted 80 degrees and spilt an estimated 400 tons of oil initially. As the spot which got ruptured in the tank was not accessible to the rescue team and the oil could not be transferred to other tanks, the Coast Guard took a conscious decision to allow the oil to flow from the two cracked tanks. The oil egress from the tanks continued for 48 hours (at a steady rate of 20 tons per hour) by which time, 60 km of the shoreline area including residential, fisheries, mangroves, ports and historic islands were polluted by the heavy oil. The total spillage was about 879 tons of oil, which travelled long distances along the shoreline of Mumbai Metropolitan region and other areas in the vicinity. In addition, tidal movement and local currents carried the crude oil along the coastlines of Alibaug, Uran, Thane, and Raigad districts. [8, 9] The island of Butcher[27] and the ancient, historic island of Elephanta[28] were also affected. Mangrove forests along the shore were covered with a slick black layer of oil. [13] The ports' (Mumbai and Jawaharlal Nehru) traffic was closed due to floating containers of oil and pesticides. Several ships and tankers waiting outside were forced to move to the outer anchorage area. Fig. 3 shows the overall region of the oil spill impact [8] and Fig. 4 is a detailed

---

[27] **Butcher Island (Jawahar Dweep)** is an island off the coast of Mumbai, India. It has an oil terminal used by the port authorities to offload it from oil tankers. The crude oil is stored in oil containers on the island. From there they are piped to Wadala, in Mumbai where they are refined. [11]

[28] The **Elephanta Caves** (natively known as **Gharapurichi Leni**) are a network of sculpted caves located on Elephanta Island, or *Gharapuri* (literally "the city of caves") in Mumbai Harbor, 10 kilometres (6.2 miles) to the east of the city of Mumbai in the Indian state of Maharashtra. The island, located on an arm of the Arabian Sea, consists of two groups of caves — a large group of five Hindu caves and a smaller group of two Buddhist caves. [12] The rock cut architecture of the caves has been dated to be between the 5th and 8th centuries, although the identity of the original builders is still a subject of debate. The caves are hewn from solid basalt rock.

Mumbai city map [15]. Most coastal districts of Maharashtra were put on high alert and ships were restricted from entering the area unless otherwise directed.

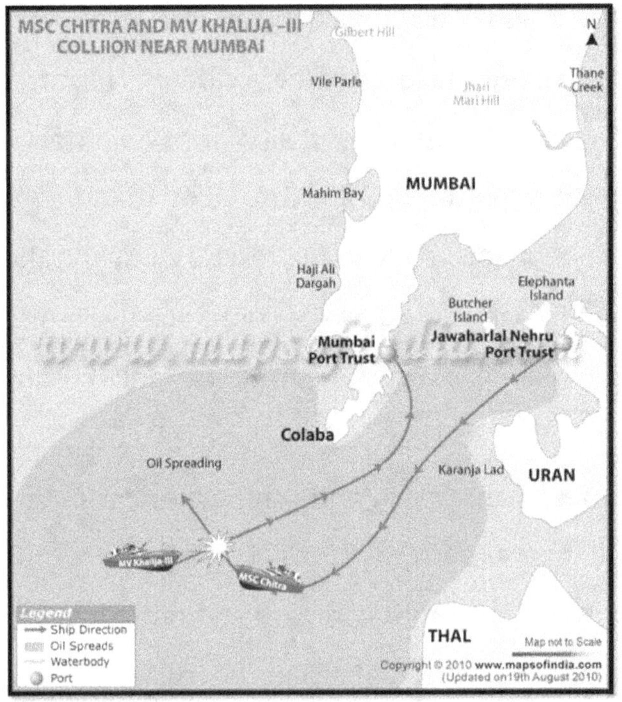

Fig. 2: MSC Chitra and MV Khalija III collision near Mumbai

On 7th of August, 2010, MSC Chitra set out from Jawaharlal Nehru Port Trust. MV Khalija III was then heading for Mumbai. These two cargo vessels collided with each other near the coast (5 nautical miles from the shore). The clash developed fractures in the body of both ships. MSC Chitra slanted after the accident resulting in a heavy oil spill. [14]

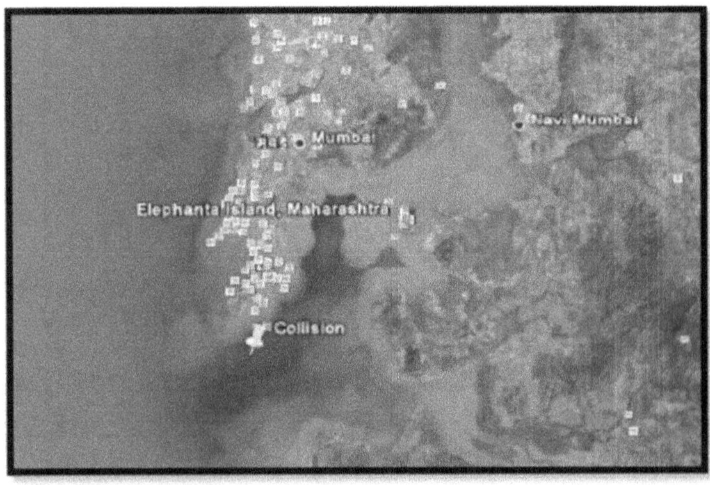

Fig. 3: Overall Area of Oil Spill Impact [8]

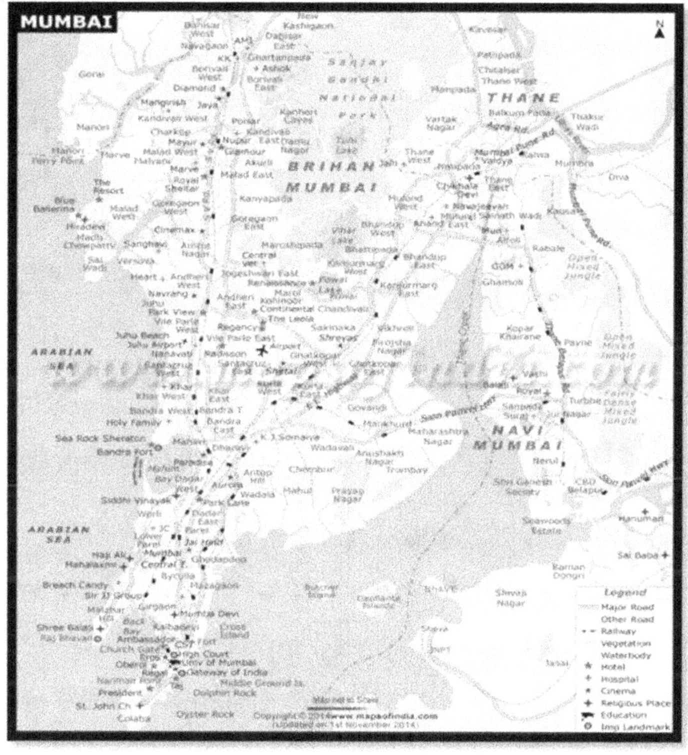

Fig. 4: Mumbai City Map [15]

V.3   CAUSE OF THE ACCIDENT

According to Coast Guard sources, the two ships were communicating on different radio frequencies; there were no pilots to guide the ships during crossings; and it is not clear if the port trust radar warned the ships. The vessel monitoring system that tracks ships was unable to establish communication between the control and captain of ships. [13, 16]

V.4 ENVIRONMENTAL IMPACT

V.4.1 IMPACT OF OIL SPILL INCIDENTS IN INDIAN COASTAL AREAS

Since the discovery of oil in India and subsequent growth of the oil industry, the country has been suffering the negative consequences of oil development.

Some of the important factors that determine how far the oil spreads, are boiling point range, pour point[29], specific gravity and viscosity etc. [17, 18] An oil spill inevitably leads to immediate spreading. The gaseous and lighter oil components evaporate completely, while a small fraction of a high boiling oil such as heavy fuel oil would evaporate, leaving behind a non-degradable residue. A thin liquid with a low pour point and low viscosity, *e.g.* petrol, would spread rapidly on the water surface aiding other weathering processes. Denser liquids having specific gravity comparable with water have a tendency to sink, especially, when associated with suspended particulate matter. Evaporation of the volatile components affects aerial life, while dissolution of the less volatile components with the resulting emulsified water affects aquatic life.

Various components of oil include *aliphatic hydrocarbons-* straight chain saturated compounds, such as methane, ethane and iso-alkanes; *alicyclic hydrocarbons-* saturated or unsaturated hydrocarbons containing 5 to 6 Carbon atoms arranged in a ring; *aromatic hydrocarbons-* may contain one, two or multiple cycles; and *non-hydrocarbons-* organic compounds containing Nitrogen, Sulfur and Oxygen and metals like Nickel, Vanadium, Copper, Zinc and Iron. [18]

The long shoreline of India has several sensitive ecosystems, such as mangroves, coral reefs, breeding and nursery grounds of marine animals and tourist beaches. [19] Spilt oil affects these ecosystems in a multitude of ways. Oil settles on beaches and kills

---

[29] The **pour point** of a liquid is the temperature at which it becomes semi solid and loses its flow characteristics. In crude oil a high **pour point** is generally associated with a high paraffin content, typically found in crude deriving from a larger proportion of plant material.

beach-dwelling organisms; oil kills flora and fauna in the estuarine zone; it settles on ocean floors and kills benthic (bottom dwelling) organisms, such as crabs and lobsters; and oil poisons algae, disrupts major food chains and decreases the yield of edible crustaceans. Fishing and Mariculture are important industries that can be affected adversely by oil spills. [20] Oil threatens fish hatcheries in coastal waters and contaminates flesh of commercially valuable fish. In addition, fishing gear and cultivation equipment may get oiled resulting in catches getting contaminated. Commercially exploited animals and plants may be harmed and seafood may get contaminated. Consumers may be reluctant to buy products from affected areas resulting in loss of market confidence and sales.

Oil gets easily absorbed by the plumage of birds and fur of animals, reducing their insulating ability, and making them more sensitive to temperature fluctuations and much less buoyant in water. [20] Oil can damage a bird's ability to fly, preventing it from foraging or running away from predators. Birds may ingest the oil coating their feathers as they preen, which can cause harm to the digestive tract, kidney and liver. A reduced foraging capacity along with damage to vital organs in the body can result in dehydration and metabolic imbalance. Some birds also experience hormonal imbalance, including alteration in their luteinizing protein.[30] Majority of birds affected by oil spills perish without human intervention. [21, 22]

There are three kinds of *oil-consuming bacteria- sulfate-reducing bacteria* (SRB) and *acid-producing bacteria* are anaerobic, while *general aerobic bacteria* (GAB) are aerobic. These bacteria occur naturally and remove oil from an ecosystem and in the process; their biomass replaces other populations in the food chain. [23]

In addition, oil spills can also cause operational problems to several coastal

---

[30] Gonadotropin (a hormone that affects function of the sex organs) is released by the pituitary gland in response to luteinizing hormone (LH)-releasing hormone. In females, LH controls the length and sequence of the female menstrual cycle, including ovulation, preparation of the uterus for implantation of a fertilized egg, and ovarian production of both estrogen and progesterone. In males, LH stimulates the testes to produce androgen [21]

industries, e.g. power plants, shipping and tourism. [5, 20] Loss of petroleum and gas, both of which are non-renewable resources, can result in their loss and lack of availability available for use. The cost of cleaning-up is also very expensive and requires a huge amount of capital. [20]

V.4.2 ENVIRONMENTAL IMPACT OF 2010 MUMBAI OIL SPILL

V.4.2.1 Field Observations

The field studies including monitoring of water quality, sediment quality, and flora and fauna at inter-tidal and sub-tidal environments were carried out four times as tabulated below (Table 2). [18]

Table 2: Sampling Series Conducted during Phase I Studies [18]

Series	Period
I	10-14 August 2010
II	18-21 August 2010
III	25-28 August 2010
IV	6-8 September 2010

Among the 15 shore transects investigated in Mumbai Bay and nearby areas on 10th august 2010 in the intertidal region, Colaba, Uran and Vashi had oil deposits of varying intensities. [18] Mangroves of Vashi and Trombay were coated with oil. Low levels of oil contamination were also found at Kihim beach. Some containers carrying teabags, biscuits and sug ar pockets were washed ashore at Dighodi and Uran. The western coast of Mumbai from Girgaon to Juhu was not affected by the spill.

The first report by the Bombay Natural History Society (BNHS) after studying the impact of the spill revealed 300 ha of lush mangroves across a 100 km stretch of the Mumbai coastline were completely destroyed. [9] Under the influence of high tide in Thane Creek, mangroves at Trombay were coated with oil up to about 0.5 to 1.0 m height. *Pneumatophores*[31], breathing roots of mangroves, and mangrove seedlings were also coated with oil in this zone. In addition, Mangroves at Vashi, JNPT, Navi Mumbai, Uran and Alibaug were found to be contaminated with oil. [9] Tar balls were found onshore in Sasvane, Kihim, Revas and Mandava along the Raigad coastline, Uran, Vashi and parts of Colaba. The damage was so severe that regeneration of Mangroves would take at least one or two years and the subsequent seeding season would show if mudflats still had the oil slick. Measures, such as bio-remediation, taken to accelerate growth would not be successful here. [9]

Elephanta Caves and Vashi were the worst affected regions in the Arabian Sea after the August 7 oil spill. The impact was so severe at Elephanta Caves that it was not clear if mangroves or marine life would revive naturally. The tidal surge at Elephanta was not strong enough to wash away the oil. [27] Inter-tidal fauna such as, small marine animals, found in shallow waters and rock crevices were primarily affected. However, the actual impact would only be known after the winter season. This is because although species spawn in the monsoon, recruitment[32] comes only after winter. The only positive factor that scientists found at some places along the coast except at Elephanta Island was the return of sensitive inter-tidal species like Fiddler crabs, *Elysia bangtawaensis* and *Haminoea vitrea*. [27, 28] The intertidal organisms including corals along the coastline of Colaba were active and alive despite the oil. [18]

In the subtidal environment, long black ribbons were seen emerging from the

---

[31]A specialized root that grows upwards out of the water or mud to reach the air and obtain oxygen for the root systems of trees that live in swampy or tidal habitats. The "knees" of mangroves and the bald cypress are pneumatophores, also called *air root*. [25]

[32] **Birth rate** or **recruitment**. Recruitment means reaching a certain size or reproductive stage. With fisheries, recruitment usually refers to the age a fish can be caught and counted in nets. [26]

ship and oriented towards the harbor. This was probably emerging from the narrow rupture site of the ship. [18] The Colaba shore was continuously coated with black oil from the seaward side. Large patches of about 500 * 100 m size having fading black color with a brownish tinge were observed drifting towards Mahul-Trombay shores. Those were probably high dispersion of oil parcels spilled on the water surface during transport. Around Trombay, the oil slick was dispersed over a larger area. At Vashi, the oil slick was seen drifting upstream at high tide and downstream at low tide. Even six days after the oil spill, a portion of the slick continued to oscillate in the Bay water with the tide.

V.4.2.2 Water Quality

V.4.2.2.1 Petroleum Hydrocarbon (PHC) content

Petroleum contamination in the coastal areas of Mumbai is a chronic problem due to anthropogenic sources such as effluents from refineries and petrochemical industries, sewage, ship traffic etc. [18] Oil is subsequently removed from the environment by several weathering processes. Therefore, concentration of PHC in water and sediment of coastal marine area of Mumbai is a net result of the quantity entering the system and is removed by weathering. This would be the *background concentration*, which should be known to analyze the post-spill levels. However, such data is missing for intertidal zones. Given intertidal areas receive land runoff during monsoons and several point sources[33] are in the vicinity, the probability of PHC levels

---

[33] A **point source** is a single identifiable *localised* source of something. Sources are called point sources because in mathematical modeling, these sources can usually be approximated as a mathematical point to simplify analysis. [29]

in intertidal waters is higher.

Test results collected during Series I showed abnormally high concentrations of PHC (1825.4-12075.6 µg/l) in the intertidal zone around the Bay mouth and at the south eastern coastal part of the Bay. The worst affected zones were Uran 1, Uran 2, Colaba and Kihim. However, Series II test results showed PHC content at Uran 1, Uran 2 and Colaba had decreased significantly (50-124.7 µg/l) and were close to the baseline. This is probably because monsoons and high tide had flushed out the oil content in water out of the Bay and scattered it widely. Therefore, the impact of accidental oil spill on affected areas was short-lived. However, during Series II measurements, Trombay area showed high levels of PHC. Since petroleum is immiscible in water, this could be a case of oil getting trapped in a confined area.

Water samples were analyzed at the mouth, Central Bay and inner segment in the subtidal zone. A wide variation of PHC content was observed ranging from 2.6 µg/l to 16902 µg/l at the three sampling sites. The water in the Central Bay showed concentrations as high as 16900 µg/l. High concentrations were particularly obtained around Butcher Island. PHC content in the Inner Bay around Vashi was 3.6 to 6684.8 µg/l. During subsequent sampling, Series II and III recorded values below 94 µg/l for all three sites. This indicates that the oil was dissolved and dispersed in water under weathering or was diluted by tidal movements and monsoons.

V.4.2.2.2 Other Water Quality Parameters (Temperature, pH, Sewage Sludge (SS), Salinity, Dissolved Oxygen (DO) and Biochemical Oxygen Demand (BOD), Nutrients, Phenols, Diurnal Variations)

Series I revealed no significant changes in SS, DO, salinity, phosphate, nitrate, nitrite, ammonia and phenols for the near shore waters or intertidal waters. [18] The only unusual variation in subtidal waters was observed in the pH range.[34] The pH varied in the range 7.1 to 8.5, which is abnormal for seawater as changes are generally in the range 7.8 to 8.3.

V.4.2.3 Sediment Quality

The Series I results in the intertidal areas revealed high concentrations of PHC at Central Bay (Trombay), Inner segment of Bay (Vashi), Coast southward of Mumbai (Mandwa, Alibaug) and Amba estuary (Dharamtar). [18] The concentration of PHCs in the sediments varied from 0.04 µg/g, wet weight to 41.1 µg/g, wet weight. Only at Colaba, levels of PHC continued to be high in the intertidal segments (35.6 µg/g, wet wt.) even during Series II measurements.

PHC concentrations for the subtidal sediments of the Mumbai Bay during Series I to III were *Not Detected (ND) to 9.1, 0.2 to 11.5 and 0.6 to 22.1 µg/g,* wet wt., respectively. Background PHC in sediments reported for Mumbai for the pre-spill period (2007-2009) was 0.2 to 10.1 µg/g, wet wt. Sediment samples from Central Bay during Series II and III showed negligible raise in PHC levels as compared to the background. Given the relatively small magnitude of the oil spill, the sinking residue was scattered by tides and monsoons, resulting in only minor settlement at the bottom sediment of a given area.

---

[34] The principal system that regulates pH of water around 7.8 to 8.3 is the carbonate system consisting of CO_2, H_2CO_3, HCO_3^-, and CO_3^{2-}. [7] In biologically active tropical water, large diurnal changes may occur (7.3 to 9.5) due to photosynthesis. The buffering system in the near shore and estuarine/creek systems, particularly during monsoons, can be affected and the pH often remains below 8. These areas are also subject to pH changes due to degradable organic matter. An oil spill may not directly induce a pH change but it may restrict photosynthesis, hence induce pH changes. [18]

V.4.2.4 Flora and Fauna

In the intertidal zone, a considerable decrease in chlorophyll a[35] (av. < 1 mg/m^3) and ratios of chlorophyll a/phaeophtin[36] (< 1) was obtained, when compared with values of September 2009. [18] This can be ascribed to the mortality of phytoplankton[37] due to increase in PHC levels in water at the shores of Uran, Trombay and Colaba. Oil spills in marine areas triggering mortality of phytoplankton is a well-studied phenomenon. [33] On the contrary, populations of zooplankton[38] and macrobenthos[39] species did not show any clear trend. Corals, barnacles, oysters and gastropods inhabiting the oil coated shore of Colaba were alive and did not show any visible signs of acute stress. The only known animal victims of the oil spill were four Indo-Pacific humpback dolphins found on the coast of Elephanta Island, Sasawne and Mandwa. [28]

In the subtidal areas, a wide variation was seen in the bacterial count of TVC[40], TC[41] and FC[42] and no particular trend was observed either in the sediment or water of Mumbai Bay. Monitoring of *chlorophyll a* and *phytoplankton* populations indicated the

---

[35] **Chlorophyll** a is a specific form of chlorophyll used in oxygenic photosynthesis. It absorbs most energy from wavelengths of violet-blue and orange-red light. It also reflects green/yellow light, and as such contributes to the observed green color of most plants. [30]

[36] **Pheophytin "a"**, a common degradation product of chlorophyll "a", can interfere with the determination of chlorophyll "a" because it absorbs light and fluoresces in the same region of the spectrum as chlorophyll "a". The **ratio of chlorophyll "a" to pheophytin "a"** serves as a good indicator of the physiological condition of phytoplankton [31]

[37] **Phytoplankton** are the autotrophic components of the plankton community and a key factor of oceans, seas and freshwater basin ecosystems. The name comes from the Greek words *phyton*, meaning "plant", and *planktos*, meaning "wanderer" or "drifter" [32]

[38] **Zooplankton** are heterotrophic plankton. Planktons are organisms drifting in oceans, seas, and bodies of fresh water. The word "zooplankton" is derived from the Greek *zoon*, meaning "animal", and *planktos*, meaning "wanderer" or "drifter" [32]

[39] **Macrobenthos** consists of the organisms that live at the bottom of a water column and are visible to the naked eye. [34]

[40] **TVC: Total Viable Count (TVC)** gives a quantitative idea about the presence of microorganisms such as **bacteria**, yeast and mold in a sample. [35]

[41] **TC:** *Coliform* **bacteria** are a commonly used bacterial indicator of sanitary quality of foods and water. They are defined as rod-shaped Gram-negative non-spore forming and motile or non-motile bacteria which can ferment lactose with the production of acid and gas when incubated at 35–37°C [36]

[42] **FC:** A *fecal coliform* (British: **faecal coliform**) is a facultatively anaerobic, rod-shaped, gram-negative, non-sporulating bacterium. *Coliform* bacteria generally originate in the intestines of warm-blooded animals. [37]

possibility of phytoplankton mortality due to oil spill in the early stages (Series I). However, rapid recovery of phytoplankton in affected areas of the Bay was observed during Series II measurements. Rapid recovery of phytoplankton in small oil spill affected areas through recruitment from unaffected adjacent sites is well known. [32]

A marked reduction (86-89%) in zooplankton *standing stock*[43] and *diversity* was evident during Series II as compared with Series I, where high PHC occurred in water. Similarly, during Series II the abundance of fish eggs and larvae decreased by 90 and 76%, respectively. Therefore, it can be concluded that the impact of oil spill on phytoplankon of the affected areas was immediate, whereas it was delayed for zooplankton.

High variability in standing stock and diversity of subtidal macrobenthos was due to substrate changes and monsoonal disturbances. There was no evidence of the impact of oil spill on the standing stock in Mumbai Bay.

The comparable levels of PHC in fish from Mumbai Bay during the pre- and post-spills rules out the possibility of bioaccumulation in fish following the oil spill.

V.4.2.5 Impact of Pesticides [18]

Some pesticide and hazardous chemicals containing metal canisters were washed ashore on the beaches. It was not clear what happened to them. Some of them spilt in the sea and resultant effects were as follows:

V.4.2.5.1 Organophosphorus Pesticides

There were canisters of three types of pesticides namely dichlorvos, acephate and quinolphos loaded on the ship. A pesticide spilt in the sea dissolves in water. Only in the localized area of spillage is the pesticide lethal to fish. Persistence of pesticides

---

[43] **Standing stock** is the weight or biomass of a stock of organisms [38]

in the Bay depends upon the mass of pesticide entering the water, rate of its dissolution, dilution by diffusion and advection etc. Being closer to marine pH, pH 9 triggers rapid hydrolysis, whereas hydrolysis is slow at pH4. Biodegradation may occur under acidic conditions with slow hydrolysis or in polluted waters, where adapted microorganisms exist.

V.4.2.5.2 Synthetic pyrethroids

A synthetic pyrethroid[44], deltamethrin, when spilled in water has a tendency to sink as the solid form is heavier than water. It is sparingly soluble in water and slowly decomposes by hydrolysis at pH > 7.5. It combines with solids and therefore, may remain in the sediment bed before being hydrolyzed. The above properties may not cause large-scale mortality of *pelagic* organisms, however, maybe of high risk to *demersal* animals at the site of the spillage[45].

V.4.2.5.3 Hazardous Chemicals

Sodium hydroxide is highly soluble in water and the dissolution process is highly exothermic. Bulk spillage of Sodium Hydroxide could increase pH and temperature of seawater and as a result, affect the biota. However, the impact would be short-lived because of the buffering capacity of seawater and rapid dispersion.

---

[44] A **pyrethroid** is an organic compound similar to the natural pyrethrins produced by the flowers of pyrethrums (*Chrysanthemum cinerariaefolium* and *C. coccineum*). Pyrethroids now constitute the majority of commercial household insecticides [39]

[45] **Pelagic fish** live in the pelagic zone of ocean or lake waters – being neither close to the bottom nor near the shore – in contrast with demersal fish that do live on or near the bottom, and reef fish that are associated with coral reefs [40]

V.4.2.6 Impact on Industries

After the Mumbai oil spill of 2010, fishing had been banned in Maharashtra for three days by the Government and civic body resulting in the loss of millions of Rupees. Around 60 fish markets across Mumbai were empty for one week and the estimated loss was Rs. 60-80 crore. The worst hit were marginal fishermen, who depend upon their daily catch for survival. About 1,100 lbs (500 kgs) of fish were contaminated with oil. [5,9]

Oil spills can also cause operational problems to several coastal industries as well as shipping. For instance, in atomic power plants, water for cooling systems is taken at a sub-surface level from the sea adjacent to the plant. If the oil floating on the surface is carried sub-surface by wave action, a potential risk exists of seawater entering the cooling water system, thereby reducing the heat transfer in steam condensors and heat exchangers causing decrease in power generation during this period. After Mumbai Oil Spill of 2010, Bhabha Atomic Research Center (BARC) was alerted not to use seawater for cooling down purposes as the oil slick had reached Sewree area, where BARC is located. [5,41]

V.5   CLEANUP AND RECOVERY

V.5.1   MANAGEMENT OF OIL SPILL INCIDENTS

A successful management of an oil spill involves not only urgent reporting of the incident but also full containment of the spill. [5] Contingency planners and other response organizations are now using Geographic Information System (GIS) to make contingency plans more convenient to use. Various advantages of using GIS are - being able to determine how to reach inaccessible oil spill sites; being able to plot maps in a GIS environment that give information about the position and size of an oil spill; being able to integrate oil drift forecast models (predicting wind and current influence on the oil spill); and being able to plan more effectively. [42]

Environmental Sensitive Index (ESI) Maps are prepared as a guideline to contingency planning to deal with oil spill problems. These maps are color coded, where the variation of colors shows the respective vulnerability of the coast. Ranking is given on a 1 to 10 scale, where 10 is assigned to highly vulnerable shores and 1 is for least vulnerable. These rankings are based on three major parameters according to National Oceanic and Atmospheric Administration (NOAA) guidelines. They are shoreline type, biological resources and human use resources. [5, 43]

Finally, creating public awareness about the impact of oil spill is an important part of managing coastal oil spills. [5]

V.5.2 CLEAN UP AND RECOVERY OF OIL SPILL INCIDENTS

Clean up and recovery of oil spills depends on a number of factors, e.g. type of oil, temperature of water (as they affect evaporation and biodegradation) and the types of shorelines and beaches involved. [44]

Various methods of cleaning up include [45]:

- *Bioremediation*: use of microorganisms or biological agents to decompose or remove the oil, e.g. *Alcanivorax*-[46] or *Methylocella Silvestris* [47]

- *Bioremediation Accelerator:* is oleophilic, hydrophobic chemical that chemically and physically bonds with both soluble and insoluble hydrocarbons. It acts as a herding agent in water by floating molecules to the surface of the water, including solubles such as phenols and BTEX[46], resulting in gel-like agglomerations. By spraying a bioremediation accelerator over sheen, the latter

---

[46] Benzene, Toluene, Ethylbenzene, and Xylene

is removed rapidly. When applied on land or on water, the nutrient-rich emulsion creates a bloom of local, indigenous, pre-existing, hydrocarbon-consuming bacteria. These bacteria break down hydrocarbons into water and carbon dioxide, with EPA tests showing 98% of alkanes biodegraded in 28 days and aromatics biodegraded 200 times faster than in nature. [48]

- *Controlled burning:* can effectively reduce the amount of oil in water [49]

- *Dispersants:* Chemical formulations composed of solvents, surfactants and other additives that disrupt the surface of an oil slick by reducing surface tension between oil and water. They consist of molecules with a hydrophilic (water-compatible) end and a lipophilic (oil-compatible) end. Dispersants link an oil droplet to water molecules and allow the natural agitation caused by winds and waves to pull droplets apart into smaller droplets. They cause the oil slick to break up and form water-soluble micelles that are rapidly diluted. [50,51]

- *Wait and watch*: Sometimes, natural attenuation works best, particularly in ecologically sensitive areas such as wetlands [52]

- *Skimming:* Floating booms can be placed around the source of the spill or at entrances to channels and harbors to reduce the spreading of an oil slick over the sea surface. Skimming is most effective in calm waters and involves various mechanisms that physically separate the oil from the water and place the oil into collection. [53]

- *Vacuum and centrifuge*: Oil can be sucked up along with water and then separated from water by centrifugation. The pure oil maybe collected in a tanker and the water returned to the sea. However, the water may contain small amounts of oil. [54]

- *Beach Raking*: Coagulated oil left on the beach maybe collected by SURF RAKE beach cleaning machines [55]

V.5.3 CLEAN UP AND RECOVERY OPERATIONS AFTER MUMBAI OIL SPILL 2010

Six coastguard vessels, a helicopter, and a small Dornier aircraft with anti-pollution dispersal spray systems were put in service to contain the oil spill. [5, 7 and 13] Fishing associations along the Maharashtra coastline were requested not to carry out any fishing activities till the emergency situation was over. Marine traffic was suspended as the oil slick was spotted two to three kilometers around the vessel Chitra and containers were sighted floating into the channel. Oil patches were seen near the islands of Elephanta and Butcher. Around 800 tons of oil was spotted floating on the sea dangerously close to the coastline. BARC was asked to stop using seawater for cooling down purposes.

The Singapore-based Smit Company was employed to salvage MSC Chitra. Equipment imported from Rotterdam and Singapore was used to suck out oil at a rate of 30 tons per hour. MSC Chitra was carrying 2662 tons of oil out of which 879 tons had flown out. In addition, there were 283.8 tons of diesel and 88,040 L of lube oil on board. It took almost 8 days to drain out the oil.

The submerged containers on the ship were removed with a crane, placed on a barge and taken to JNPT. Simultaneously, the ship's tanks were filled with water to prevent it from losing balance.

The oil washed ashore also polluted shoreline areas and Mumbai's beaches that are major tourist attractions. To clean up the beaches, Maharashtra Pollution Control Board (MPCB) took the services of The Energy and Resources Institute (TERI), which has developed a certain mixture of oil-zapping bacteria. The concoction of oil-zapping bacteria was developed by TERI over a period of seven years and the project was funded by Department of Biotechnology and Ministry of Science and Technology. [56]

The Oil zapper is a mixture of five different bacterial strains that are immobilized and *combined with a carrier material (powdered corncob). The Oil zapper feeds on hydrocarbon compounds present in crude oil and oily sludge (a hazardous hydrocarbon waste generated by oil refineries) and converts them into harmless CO_2 and water. The Oil zapper is packed into sterile polythene bags and sealed aseptically for safe transport. The shelf life of the product is three months at ambient temperature.*

This technology has been used successfully in treating 130,000 tons of oily sludge or oil contaminated soil and is being used by almost all leading oil companies in India. Although bioremediation is the ideal process to treat oil-contaminated sludge, it does produce carbon dioxide. The rate and amount of carbon dioxide produced determines the extent of damage it can cause.

V.6   LESSONS LEARNT

Several lessons can be drawn from the MSC Chitra oil spill accident. The Coast Guard was ill-equipped to contain the oil spill in the fast tidal current as the pollution response equipment available was not sufficiently compatible. The shoreline terrain was rocky and the inshore boom[47] was not useful. There is a need for deflection booms for effective protection of mangroves. The vessels deployed for response require modification to transport pollution response equipment for skimming (see Section V.2) operations. [7]

The local State Government is ill-equipped to prevent or contain the spill or undertake shoreline clean-up. The contingency plan prepared by ports and oil handling agencies cannot handle more than 100 tons of oil at a time. There are no private oil spill response providers to undertake oil spill response on behalf of the port. Therefore,

---

[47] **Booms** are large floating barriers that round up oil and lift the oil off the water [49]

proposals were made to increase the pollution response capacity of the ports by the Ministry through the Oil Cess Fund.

V.7 SUMMARY

On 7th August, 2010, MSC Chitra setting out from JNPT collided with MV Khalija III, which was heading towards Mumbai. Both were cargo vessels and collided at 5 nautical miles from the shore. MSC Chitra was loaded with 2,600 tons of oil and 31 containers of pesticides. The impact of the collision was so severe that the two fuel tanks on the port side of MV Chitra were fractured; the ship tilted 80 degrees and spilt an estimated 400 tons of oil initially. The crack in the fuel tanks led to continuous outpour of oil for 48 hours. Overall 879 tons of oil scattered widely along the Mumbai Metropolitan shoreline and other neighboring areas. Tidal movements and local currents carried the oil further along the coastlines of Alibaug, Uran, Thane, and Raigad. The environmental impact of oil on the quality of water, sediments and flora and fauna has also been discussed. A section on management and cleanup of oil spills in general and how the Mumbai 2010 spill was managed has also been included.

6 LESSONS LEARNT

THE KEY PHILOSOPHY of ancient Indian civilization was to live in harmony with nature and cosmic principles. This included all spheres of life, like, urban planning, architecture, medicine, surgery etc. With the advent of the Industrial Revolution in the mid-eighteenth century, issues like air, water pollution, sanitation and hygiene became serious concerns. In the post-war era, it was Rachel Carson's book, *The Silent Spring that* gave birth to contemporary 'environmentalism' in 1962. The book highlighted how DDT (considered a miracle compound at that time) moved up in the food chain and did not biodegrade easily. Apart from a ban on several deadly Persistent Organic Pollutants (POPs), the book generated a larger interest in society about environmental problems, e.g., air pollution and oil spills. As a result of several eminent thinkers and scientists, it is now widely recognized that development is important but so is 'environmental preservation'. 'Sustainability' and 'sustainable development' have become the key terms for modern environmentalists.

To illustrate these two concepts, four case studies on disasters concerning water resource management were discussed in detail. Two of these case studies –Minimata Disease and Love Canal- took place in developed countries and the incidents lasted approximately an entire century. Both events are intertwined with the respective histories of the countries where they took place and it took decades before the full extent of the pollution was realized. Whereas Baia Mare and Mumbai Oil Spill are more recent occurrences that happened in developing countries due to human and technical errors.

The story of the growth of Chisso Company also coincides with the rise of imperialism in Japan. It is, therefore, not surprising that the company zealous to build its technological prowess employed highly qualified, cheap labor and was quick to adapt new albeit dangerous technologies. As the II World War approached, the demand for petroleum-derived products for consumption by the military increased. Since Japan did not have access to natural petroleum resources, Chisso quickly developed alternative pathways to obtain similar product *via* the use of acetylene chemistry. It is this high technology combined with the samurai spirit that helped Chisso emerge like a mythical phoenix when it lost all its overseas assets after the II World War.

The production of acetaldehyde required acetylene to be blown over Mercuric sulfate. The process generated a lot of waste Mercury all of which was disposed in Minamata Bay without treatment. This first affected the fish in the bay and then through the food chain, higher organisms, e.g. cats and finally, human beings.

With hindsight, the cause of the Minimata disease is clear. However, it took several years of research before the reason of the strange disease could be traced to Mercury. Another factor that prevented the discovery of the problem was the feudal structure of Japanese society. Chisso, both as the provider and protector of the town's workforce had taken over the role of patriarchal landlord from feudal Japan. It was not so easy for the people to blame openly the company or for the company to admit its 'guilt'.

Love Canal is the account of an abandoned canal that was originally dug to connect Niagara River and Lake Ontario in order to increase the supply of hydroelectricity in the region. In the 1920s, the canal became a dumpsite for municipal refuse. In the 1940s, Hooker Electrochemical Company was granted permission by the Niagara Power and Development Company to dump their chemical waste in the Love Canal. In addition, the City of Niagara Falls and the US army also dumped their refuse in the canal. The landfill site was in operation till 1953 after which, it was covered with soil and vegetation.

In 1953, the site was sold to the City of Niagara Falls Board of Education, New York for $1. Hooker Chemical on its part made sure that the School had been forewarned and absolved itself of future repercussions by including in the deed a disclaimer of responsibility for any damages due to the buried chemicals. In its eagerness to build schools for the growing population, the School Board failed to fully comprehend the dangers that lay underneath the land on which they wanted to build. This eagerness, however, could also be ascribed to the urgent demand for land due to an increase in population. Two schools were constructed on this site by the Board and the remaining land was sold for homes to be built by private developers and the Housing Authority. During construction of the school and houses, the clay lining of the landfill was severely tampered with. The unusually high precipitation of 1975 and 1976 resulted in high groundwater levels in the Love Canal area. *It is worth highlighting here that 'groundwater' here refers to subsurface water and not water in bedrock aquifers.* The clay lining had been washed away revealing 55 gallon drums. Basements were oozing an oily residue, sump pumps were corroded and the area was filled with noxious odors. This is when the forgotten landfill site came into light and the matter became public.

There were several reports of birth defects, enlarged feet, heads, hands and legs, miscarriages, unexplained illnesses and mental retardation.

From 1979 to 2004, it took 24 years for the site to be cleaned up. Compensation was given by the State to the victims. The most important outcome of the incident was the Superfund Act that required clean-up of sites contaminated with hazardous substances.

Both the above case studies demonstrate how human actions triggered by ambition or entrepreneurship without proper planning can have long-lasting and dangerous implications for future generations. In its zeal for technological progress, Chisso failed to test the hazards associated with the use of Mercury or other heavy metals while the City of Niagara School Board failed to fully comprehend the hazards of building schools on a former landfill.

The nature of the society in which the disaster takes place also has an impact on the outcome.   The feudal structure of Japanese society hampered recognition of Minimata disease, which carried a lot of prejudice and stigma with it and compensation was slow to come.   The US being a more open society was quick to respond with emergency funding, relocation, compensation and site clean-up once the hazards were recognized.   Clean-up of both sites was expensive and lengthy.   Both countries responded with appropriate litigation to safeguard their respective populations from future repetitions.

The Baia Mare incident happened in Maramures County, rich in minerals- Gold, Silver, Copper, Lead and salt and is historically known for mining. There is a high level of chronic ground, water and air pollution due to several decades of industrial activity in the region without any appropriate waste treatment.   In this backdrop, Aurul Company started its operations in May 1999 of mining residues of former gold and silver extraction processes. Aurul was a joint venture between the Australian company Esmeralda Exploration and the Romanian Government. According to the arrangement, Aurul would earn profits from its mining operations and Romanian authorities would benefit from Aurul's management and cleaning up of Baia Mare's old contaminated ponds. Aurul had obtained all necessary environmental permits required by Romanian law for its plant in Baia Mare.   Nevertheless there were several problems in the operation of the system– extensive network of unprotected pipelines; toxic seepage due to lack of liner in the old Meda pond; no precaution to deal with a puncture; dam design was faulty with respect to quantity of coarse material; and hydrocyclones that separate tailings from toxic water were not operating at low temperatures.   When the spill happened, they were not in operation for a week.   In addition, precipitation and evaporation was not being monitored.

A year after Aurul started its operations in January, 2000, an unusually high amount of precipitation in the Baia Mare area led to accumulation of excess water in the dam and eventually caused a break in the dam surrounding the tailings pond. The accident led to release of 100,000 m^3 of cyanide – contaminated water and suspended waste that initially flowed into Sasar River. Travelling through a network of rivers, the cyanide plume spread into Romania, Hungary and Federal Republic of Yugosla*via*. Phytoplankton and zooplankton communities were entirely destroyed wherever the cyanide plume passed and about 1240 tons of fish were killed in the Tisza River.

The United Nations Environment Program-Office for the Coordination of Humanitarian Affairs- prepared a comprehensive report assessing the situation and giving a list of recommendations for future preparedness. Some of those recommendations included public awareness; environmental impact assessment of mining operations; more rigorous sampling and analyses; improvement in drinking water; broader environment management and sustainable development plan for Maramures County and Tisza River Catchment area; and finally, liability and compensation for the cyanide spill affected victims.

The last case study is about spilling of oil off the coast of Mumbai 5 nautical miles from the shore in 2010, when MSC Chitra setting out from Jawaharlal Nehru Port Trust collided with MV Khalija III heading towards Mumbai. There has been a long history of oil spills along the Indian coast. Oil spills can occur during transportation of oil; ship accidents; various phases of production, *e.g.* when oil is being extracted from an oil well or being converted into other products at a refinery; offshore drilling; weapon of war; or illegal dumping.

The impact of the collision was so severe that the two fuel tanks on the port side were ruptured and 400 tons of oil split initially. The oil egress continued for 48 hours and the total spillage was estimated to be about 879 tons. 60 km of shoreline area including residential, fisheries, mangroves, ports and historic islands were contaminated by the heavy oil.

Six coastguard vessels, a helicopter and a small Dornier aircraft were employed to spray anti-pollution dispersants along the Maharashtra coastline. In addition, oil was also sucked out at 30 tons/hour. The oil washed ashore was cleaned up with indigenously developed 'oil zapping' bacterial mixture.

The latter two incidents are more recent occurrences and took place in developing countries. However, they were not isolated events nor were they totally unpredictable. In Romania, despite decades of being exposed to industrial and mining activity, society is not so vociferous about environmental deterioration. Oil spills have also been occurring along the Indian coastline for several decades yet there has been no public outcry to prevent or contain them. In both cases, comprehensive environment impact assessment reports are missing and there are limitations in technology and manpower to prevent or contain the incidents. The question of liability and compensation has been discussed but yet to be implemented. Most importantly, despite such large-scale damage, no litigation has resulted out of the two events.

BIBLIOGRAPHY

CHAPTER 1

1) Baez, A. V., Knamiller, G. W., & Smyth, J. C. (Eds.).*The Environment and Science and Technology Education*; Permagon Press for ICSU Press: Oxford, U.K., 1987.

2) Bussey, M., Inayatullah, S., Milojevi, I., *Alternative Educational Futures: Pedagogies for Emergent Worlds*; Rotterdam: Sense Publishers, 2008, pp 235-252.

3) Ravindranath, M. J. Environmental education in teacher education in India: experiences and challenges in the United Nation's Decade of Education for Sustainable Development. *Journal of Education for Teaching: International Research and Pedagogy,* **2007**, 33(2), 191–206.

4) Sarabhai, K. *Strategy for Environmental Education: An Approach for India*. Paper presented at the North American Association for Environmental Education, 1995.

5) Singh, R.P. Environmental Concerns (The Vedas)-A Lesson in Ancient Indian History, *Shaikshik Parisamvad (An International Journal of Education)- SPIJE*, 2011. **1(1).**

6) Renugadevi, R. Environmental Ethics in the Hindu Vedas and Puranas in India, *African Journal of History and Culture,* **2012**, 4(1), 1-3.

7) Tiwari, S. Origin of Environmental Science from the Vedas. http://www.sanskrit.nic.in/svimarsha/v2/c17.pdf (accessed November 28, 2015).

8)   Sarmah, R. Environmental Awareness in the Vedic Literature: An assessment, *International Journal of Sanskrit Research*, **2015**, *1(4)*, 5-8.

9)   Misra, V.N. *Creativity and Environment*; Sahitya Academy: New Delhi, India, 1992.

10)   Sharma, K.N. (2009, June 30). Vedic perspective on environment. *Times of India*. Retrieved from http://timesofindia.indiatimes.com/life-style/; Sharma, K.N. (2010, October 29). Vedic perspective on environment. *Times of India*. Retrieved from http://www.speakingtree.in/article/

11)   Desai, F.P. Ecological Ethics In Vedic Metaphysics An Effectual Method To Indoctrinate Environmental Awareness, *Journal of Environmental Research and Development*, **2009**, *4(2)*, 636-642.

12)   Rajani Rao, U. Environmental awareness in ancient India. *International Journal of Life Sciences Research*, **2014**, *2(2)*, pp. 1-7; Rajendran, C. Environmental awareness in ancient India.   In *Does environmental history matter? : shikar, subsistence, sustenance and the sciences*; Chakrabarti, R., Ed; Readers Service: Kolkata, India, 2006.

13)   Wordsworth, W. *A guide through the district of the lakes in the north of England with a description of the scenery, &c. for the use of tourists and residents,* 5th ed.; Hudson and Nicholson: Kendal, England, 1835; pp 88.

14)   Barberis, P., McHugh, J., Tyldesley, M., *Encyclopedia of British and Irish Political Organizations. Parties, Groups and Movements of the 20th Century*, Revised Ed; A&C Black, 2000.

15)   The Life and Contributions of John Muir. http://vault.sierraclub.org/john_muir_exhibit/life/ (accessed November 27, 2015).

16) Furtak, Rick Anthony, "Henry David Thoreau", *The Stanford Encyclopedia of Philosophy* (Fall 2014 Edition), Edward N. Zalta (ed.), http://plato.stanford.edu/archives/fall2014/entries/thoreau/ (accessed November 27 2015).

17) Thoreau, H.D., *Walden or Life in the Woods, Ticknor and Fields: Boston,* 1854.

18) Carson, R. *Silent Spring.* Houghton Mifflin: Boston, U.S.A., 1962.

19) Greenpeace International. http://www.greenpeace.org/international/en/ (accessed November 27 2015); Weyler, R., The Greenpeace Book. http://rexweyler.com/greenpeace/greenpeace-history/chronology/ (accessed November 27 2015).

20) Friends of the Earth. http://www.foe.org/ (accessed November 27 2015).

21) Ward, B., Dubois, R., Strong, M.F. *Only One Earth: The Care and Maintenance of a Small Planet*; W. W. Norton & Company: New York, U.S.A., 1972.

22) Suter, K. The Club of Rome: The Global Conscience. *Contemporary Review*, **1999**, *275 (1602)*, 1-5; The Club of Rome. http://www.clubofrome.org/ (accessed November 27 2015).

23) Behrens III, W.W.; Randers, J.; Meadows, D.; Meadows, D. *Limits to Growth*, Universe Books, 1972.

24) Earth Day: The History of a Movement. http://www.earthday.org (accessed November 27 2015).

25) Baylis, J.; Smith, S. *The Globalization of World Politics,* 3rd ed.; Oxford University Press: Oxford, 2005, pp.454-455.

26) Lovelock, J.E. Gaia as seen through the atmosphere. *Atmospheric Environment,* **1972**, *6(8)*, 579–580; Lovelock, J.E.; Margulis, L. Atmospheric homeostasis by and for the biosphere: the Gaia hypothesis. *Tellus Series A: Dynamic Meteorology and*

Oceanography, **1974**, *26(1–2),* 2–10.; Turney, J. *Lovelock and Gaia: Signs of Life;* Icon Books: UK, 2003.

27) Almeida, S.; Cutter-Mackenzie, A. The Historical, Present and Future *ness* of Environmental Education in India. *Australian Journal of Environmental Education,* **2011**, *27(1),* 122-133.

28) Rangarajan, M., Ed. *Environmental Issues in India: A Reader;* Dorling Kindersley (India) Pvt. Ltd: New Delhi, India, 2009; Ravindranath, M. J. Living Traditions. In Yencken, D.; Fien, J.; Sykes, H., Eds. *Environment, Education and Society in the Asia-Pacific: local traditions and global discourses;* Routledge: London, U.K., 2000.

29) Sarabhai, K.; Raghunathan, M.; Kandula, K. *Status Reports: India.,* 2000; Center for Environmental Education: Ahmedabad, India.

30) WWF Envis Center on NGOs and Parliament, Directory of Environmental NGOs in India. http://www.wwfenvis.nic.in/directory_NGO.aspx (accessed November 27, 2015).

31) (2010, September 27). Eco-Ganesha celebrates city's new green spirit. *Daily News & Analysis.* Retrieved from http://www.dnaindia.com/mumbai/report_eco-ganesha-celebrates city's-new-green-spirit_1443832

32) Bharucha, E. *Textbook for Environmental Studies for Undergraduate Courses of All Branches of Higher Education;* University Grants Commission and Bharati Vidyapeeth Institute of Environmental Education and Research: New Delhi, India, 2004, pp 9-11.

33) Luce, E. *In Spite of the Gods: The Strange Rise of Modern India;* Little, Brown Group: London, U.K., 2006; Kamdar, M. *Planet India: The Turbulent Rise of The Largest Democracy and The Future Of Our World;* cribner: New York, U.S.A., 2007.

34) Cutter-Mackenzie, A. Teaching for sustainability. In Gilbert, R.; Hoepper, B., (Eds.), *Teaching Society and Environment,* 4th Ed.; Cengage Learning: South Melbourne, Australia, 2010, pp. 348–363.

35) Chhokar, K. B. Higher education and curriculum innovation for sustainable development in India. *International Journal of Sustainability in Higher Education,* **2010**, *11*(2), 141–152; Joshi, M. *ESD in India: Current Practices and Development Plans.* Paper presented at the International Conference on Education for Sustainable Development 2005; Kuching, Sarawak, Malaysia, 2005; Khirwadkar, A., Pushpanadam, K. Education for Sustainable Development :Implications for Teacher Education. *International Forum of Teaching and Studies,* 2007, *3(3),* 5–13.

CHAPTER 2

1.   Davis, J. Toxic, Persistent Chemicals in Human Environments: Case Studies of Agent Orange Use in Vietnam, 1965-1970 and Methyl Mercury in Minamata Bay, Japan, 1932-1968. Yale National Initiative to strengthen teaching in public schools. http://teachers.yale.edu/curriculum/viewer/initiative (accessed December 16, 2015).

2.   Allchin D., The Poisoning of Minimata. https://www1.umn.edu/ships/ethics/minamata.htm (accessed December 16, 2015).

3.   Minimata Disease Municipal Museum (Ed.) *Minimata Disease- Its History and Lessons*; Minimata City Planning Division: Minimata, Japan, 2007.

4.   Kurtenbach, E. (1989, June 18) Minimata heals slowly in the wake of poison deaths. *The Milwaukee Journal.* Retrieved from https://news.google.com/newspapers

5.   The Shiranui Sea is a small and calm sea, Exhibition of Minimata disease Museum. http://www.soshisha.org (accessed December 16, 2015).

6.   Allen, K.; Burns, C. (2009). Minamata Disease. In *Encyclopedia of Earth.* Retrieved from http://www.eoearth.org/view/article/154624

7.   Withrow S.J.; Vail, D.M. *Withrow and MacEwen's Small Animal Clinical Oncology;.* Illustrated; Elsevier Heath Sciences, 2007, p. 73-4.

8.   A wide range of disabilities from daily life, Exhibition of Minimata disease Museum. http://www.soshisha.org (accessed December 16, 2015).

9.   Ui, J., Ed. *Industrial Pollution in Japan*; United Nations University Press: Tokyo, Japan, 1992.

10. Almeida, P; and Stearns, L. Political opportunities and local grassroots environmental movement: The case of Minamata. *Social Problems* **1998,** *45(1)*, 37–60.

11. Mercury was used to produce acetaldehyde, Exhibition of Minimata disease Museum. http://www.soshisha.org (accessed December 16, 2015).

12. Report of the Social Scientific Study Group on Minamata Disease. (2001) *In the Hope of Avoiding Repetition of a Tragedy of Minamata Disease-what we have learned from the experience.* National Institute for Minamata Disease.

13. Eto, K., Marumoto, M. and Takeya, M. (2010) The pathology of methylmercury poisoning (Minamata disease). *Neuropathology.* **2010,** *30(5),* 471-479.

14. Nabi, S. *Toxic Effects of Mercury,* illustrated; Springer, 2014.

15. Gilhooly, R. (2015, June 13) Mercury rising: Niigata struggles to bury its Minimata ghosts, *Japan Times.* Retrieved from http://www.japantimes.co.jp/news/2015/06/13/national/history

16. Benesch, O. *Inventing the Way of the Samurai: Nationalism, Internationalism, and Bushido in Modern Japan;* Oxford University Press: Oxford, U.K., 2014.

17. Barnhart, R.K., Ed. (1995) *Phoenix.* The Barnhart Concise Dictionary of Etymology. Harper Collins, New York.

18. Harada, M. *Minamata Disease;* Iwanami Shoten Publishers: Tokyo, Japan, 1972.

19. Methyl Mercury drains out of Chisso into the Sea, Exhibition of Minimata disease Museum. http://www.soshisha.org (accessed December 16, 2015).

20. Timothy, G.S. *Minamata: Pollution and the Struggle for Democracy in Postwar Japan, Harvard East Asian Monographs Book 194;* Harvard University Press: Cambridge, U.S.A, 2001.

21. Smith, W. E.; Smith, A.M. *Minamata: Words and Photographs;* Holt, Rinehart and Winston: New York, U.S.A., 1975.

22.   Gilbert, S., Minimata, Japan. http://www.toxipedia.org/display/toxipedia/ (accessed December 16, 2015)

23.   Gilbert, S. G. A Small Dose of Toxicology: The Health Effects of Common Chemicals; CRC Press, Taylor and Francis Group, 2004.

24.   Dartmouth Toxic Metals, Superfund Research Program, Why Mercury? http://www.dartmouth.edu/~toxmetal/mercury/ (accessed December 16, 2015).

25.   Bioaccumulation, Environment Health-Toxic Substances, USGS. http://toxics.usgs.gov/definitions/bioaccumulation.html (accessed December 16, 2015).

26.   Biomagnification, Environment Health-Toxic Substances, USGS, http://toxics.usgs.gov/definitions/biomagnification.html (accessed December 16, 2015).

27.   Mercury travels from fish and shellfish to man, Exhibition of Minimata disease Museum. http://www.soshisha.org (accessed December 16, 2015).

28.   Ishimare, M, Livia, M. *Paradise in the sea of sorrow: Our Minimata Disease*; University of Michigan Center: Ann Arbor, U.S.A., 2003.

CHAPTER 3

1. National Institute for Research and Development in Informatics, Bucharest, Romania. http://romania.ici.ro/ (accessed December 12, 2015); Municipiul Baia Mare. http://www.baiamare.ro/ro/ (accessed December 12, 2015); Maramures Guide http://maramuresguide.com/about_maramures/geography/ (accessed December 12, 2015).

2. Maramures Baia Mare. http://www.worldheritage.org/ (accessed December 12, 2015).

3. United Nations Environment Program/Office for the Coordination of Humanitarian Affairs. (2000) *Cyanide Spill at Baia Mare Romania, Spill of liquid and suspended waste at the Aurul S.A. Retreatment Plant at Baia Mare.* Geneva: Regional Office for Europe.

4. Discover Romania, The Chestnut festival of Baia Mare city. https://discoveringromania.wordpress.com/ (accessed December 12, 2015).

5. Ezilon maps, Europe maps. http://www.ezilon.com/maps/europe-maps (accessed December 14, 2015).

6. Maramures Road Map. http://www.romanianmonasteries.org/maramuresmap1.html (accessed December 14, 2015).

7. RES Champions League, Best Practices, Baia Mare is determined to act for a better future. http://www.res-league.eu/eng/ (accessed December 12, 2015).

8. Monbiot, G. (2010, May 19). Romania's poison dump. *BBC.* Retrieved from http://news.bbc.co.uk/

9.   Csagoly, P. (2000) *The Cyanide Spill at Baia Mare, Romania, Before, During and After.* Geneva: The Regional Environmental Center for Central and Eastern Europe.

10.   Allaby, A.; Allaby, M. "tailings dam." <u>A Dictionary of Earth Sciences</u>. 1999. Retrieved December 14, 2015 from Encyclopedia.com: http://www.encyclopedia.com/doc/1O13-tailingsdam.html

11.   Bournay, E., UNEP/GRID-Ardenal (2006). Industrial hotspots Tisza River Basin. *Economic and Poverty Times # 3. Disaster Issue.* Retrieved from http://www.grida.no/publications/et; United Nations Environment Program. (2004) *Rapid Environmental Assessment of the Tisza River Basin.* Geneva: UNEP Regional Office for Europe and UNEP/DEWA/GRID~Europe.

12.   Kovac, C. Cyanide spill could have long-term impact. *British Medical Journal.* **2000**, *320*, 1294.

13.   Report of the International Task for assessing the Baia Mare Accident, World Wildlife Fund Global. http://www.wwf.panda.org/ (accessed December 14, 2015)

14.   Pérez del Postigo Prieto, N. (2014) *Stability Analysis of Dam Failures. Application to Aurul Tailing Pond in Baia Mare (Romania)*, Ph.D. Thesis. Retrieved from http://www.oa.upm.es (Accession no. 32788/1/PFC).

15.   Cyanide Leach Mining Packet, *Mineral Policy Center*, Washington DC, 2000. http://www.mineralpolicy.org (accessed December 14, 2015).

16.   Hoffman, J.E. (2015) Gold Processing. In *Encyclopedia Britannica*. Retrieved from http://www.britannica.com

17.   Theodore, M.G.; Gong, T.R. (2014) Ore leaching method for metals recovery. *US Patent No. 8,888,890 B2*. Washington D.C.: US Patent and Trademark Office.

18. Van Zyl, D.J.A.; Hutchison, I.P.G.; Kiel, J.E., Eds. *Introduction to Evaluation, Design and Operation of Precious Metal Heap Leaching Projects*, illustrated; Society of Mining Engineers: U.S.A., 1988, pp 122-145.

19. Hydrocyclone working principle, New Technologies. http://newtech.dp.ua/articles/eng/ (accessed December 14, 2015).

20. Buha, A; Williams, M.M. Baia Mare Cyanide Spill. http://www.toxipedia.org (accessed December 14, 2015).

21. MTI, Ministry for Environmental Protection (Hungary) Environmental Inspectorate, UNEP.

22. Dam Safety Scheme in Guidance for regional authorities and owners of large dams, Building Performance. http://www.building.govt.nz (accessed December 14, 2015).

23. Balkau, F. Learning from Baia Mare. *Environment and Poverty Times*, **2005**, *3*, 44-45.

24. Thurman, H. V. *Introductory Oceanography*; Prentice Hall College: New Jersey, USA, 1997.

25. (2004, December 13). Map: Pollution hotspots. *BBC News*. Retrieved from http://news.bbc.co.uk/2/hi/science/nature; (2000, March 14). Hungary demands action over pollution. *BBC News*. Retrieved from http://news.bbc.co.uk/2/hi/europe/; (2001, January 31). One Year On: Romania's Cyanide Spill. *BBC News*. Retrieved from http://news.bbc.co.uk/2/hi/europe

CHAPTER 4

1. University at Buffalo Libraries. Background Information, Love Canal Collections. http://library.buffalo.edu/specialcollections/lovecanal/ (accessed December 21, 2015).

2. Geneseo History Department, The State University of New York. Love Canal - A Brief History. https://www.geneseo.edu/history/love_canal_history (accessed December 21, 2015).

3. Angelo, L. (2008). Love Canal, New York. Retrieved from http://www.eoearth.org/view/article/154300

4. United States Environmental Protection Agency. (1982) *Environmental Monitoring at Love Canal, Volume 1*. (EPA-600/4-82-030a). Washington, DC: Office of Research and Development.

5. Kluessendorf, J. (October 2010). A Look at the Ledge. *A Wisconsin Natural Resources Magazine*. Retrieved from http://dnr.wi.gov/wnrmag/2010/10/ledge.htm

6. Welby, C.W.; Gowan, M.E. *A Paradox of Power: Voices of Warning and Reason in the Geosciences*; Reviews in Engineering Geology; Geological Society of America: U.S.A., 1998.

7. "Map of Niagara Falls, N.Y. highlighting the Love Canal site," *Digital Collections*, accessed July 31, 2015, http://digital.lib.buffalo.edu/items/show/16234

8. William Love and a Model City in Lewiston, N.Y. Parry; "William T. Love and the Development of a Model City," 1976, 19.11, Mss. C94-2, Adeline Levine Love Canal Collection, 1893-1995 (bulk 1978-1995), Research Library, Buffalo History

Museum. Retrieved from http://purl.org/net/findingaids/view?docId=ead/bechs/bechs_c94_2.xml

9.   Ploughman, P. Love Canal; Arcadia Publishing: U.S.A., 2013.

10.   Levine, A. G. *Love Canal: Science, Politics and People*; D.C. Heath and Company: Lexington, MA, 1982.

11.   Blum, E. D. *Love Canal Revisited: Race, Class, and Gender in Environmental Activism*; University Press of Kansas: Kansas, U.S.A., 2008, p.21.

12.   Berton, P. *Niagara: a history of the falls*; Excelsior Editions/State University of New York: U.S.A., 2009.

13.   Colten, C. E.; Skinner, P. N. *The Road to Love Canal: Managing Industrial Waste Before EPA*; University of Texas Press: Austin, Texas, U.S.A., 1996.

14.   University of Buffalo Libraries. Chronologies, Love Canal Collections. http://library.buffalo.edu/specialcollections/lovecanal/ (accessed December 21, 2015).

15.   University of Buffalo Libraries. History of Disaster at Love Canal, Chronology of Events. http://library.buffalo.edu/specialcollections/lovecanal/documents/pdfs/etf_chron1.pdf (accessed December 21, 2015).

16.   "Love Canal." International Encyclopedia of the Social Sciences. 2008. Retrieved December 21, 2015 from Encyclopedia.com: http://www.encyclopedia.com/doc/1G2-3045301389.html

17.   Zuesse, E. *Love Canal: The Truth Seeps Out*; Reason Enterprises: U.S.A., 1981.

18.   Richard L. Stroup. "Free-Market Environmentalism." *The Concise Encyclopedia of Economics*. 2008. Library of Economics and Liberty. Retrieved December 22, 2015 from the World Wide Web: http://www.econlib.org/library/Enc/FreeMarketEnvironmentalism.html

19.   Brown, M. *Laying Waste: The Poisoning of America by Toxic Chemicals;* Washington Square Press: New York, 1981.

20.   Beck, E. C. (1979) The Love Canal Tragedy. *EPA Journal.* Retrieved from http://www.epa.gov/history/topics/lovecanal/01.htm

21.   Gensburg, L.J.; Pantea, C.I.; Fitzgerald, E.F.; Stark, A.; Kim, N. Mortality among former Love Canal residents. *Environ Health Perspect.,* **2009,** *117,* 209–216.

22.   Pelclova, D.; Urban, P.; Preiss, J.; Lukás, E.; Fenclová, Z.; Navrátil, Z.; Dubská, Z.; Senholdová, Z. Adverse health effects in humans exposed to 2,3,7,8-tetrachlorodibenzo-*p*-dioxin (TCDD). *Rev. Environ. Health,* **2006,** *21(2);* 119-38.

23.   Board on Environmental Studies and Toxicology, Committee on Environmental Epidemiology, National Research Council, Division on Earth and Life Studies, Commission on Life Sciences. *Environmental Epidemiology, Volume 1: Public Health and Hazardous Wastes;* National Academies Press: Washington, D.C., 1991.

24.   Center for Health, Environment and Justice. (n.d.) Love Canal. Retrieved from http://chej.org/wp-content/uploads/Documents/love_canal_factpack.pdf

25.   Love Canal Superfund Site, Sevenson Environmental Services Inc.. http://www.sevenson.com/index.php/project-summaries/love-canal-superfund-site/ (accessed December 22, 2015).

26.   Jordan, M. *Hush Hush: The Dark Secrets of Scientific Research;* Firefly Books: Buffalo, U.S.A., 2003, p.108.

27.   Sector, B. (2004, Sept. 30). EPA removes Love Canal from Superfund list. Retrieved Dec. 1, 2011, from http://www.epa.gov/superfund/accomp/news/lovecanal.htm

28.   P.L. 96-510, 42 U.S.C.& (33).html § 9601(14) & (33), December 11, 1980.

29.   U.S. v. Hooker Chemicals and Plastics Corp., 850 Federal Supplement, 993 (W.D.N.Y., 1994)

30.   Parrish, M. (1994, June 22). Occidental to pay $129 Million in Love Canal Settlement. *Los Angeles Times.* Retrieved from http://articles.latimes.com/1994-06-22/business/fi-7158_1_love-canal-site

CHAPTER 5

1.   Gouda, R.; Panigrahy, R.C. Phytoplankton in Indian estuaries, *J. Indian Ocean Studies*, **1999**, *7(1)*, 74-82.

2.   Grainger, R.; Garcia, S.M. Fisheries management and sustainability: A new perspective of an old problem. *World Fisheries Congress*, Brisbane, Australia, 28 July-2 August, 1996.

3.   Dyer, K.R.; Christe, M.C.; and Wright, E.W. The classification of mudflats. *Cont. Shelf Res.*, 2000, **20**, 1061-1078; Stutz, M. L.; Pilkey, O. H. Global distribution and morphology of deltaic barrier island systems. *J. Coast. Res.* **2002**. *36*, 694-707.

4.   India States and Capitals. http://www.mapsofindia.com (accessed December 8, 2015).

5.   Rai, N.; Pandey, I.P.; Joshi, K. Impacts and Management of Oil Spill Pollution along the Indian Coastal Areas, *J.Ind.Res.Tech.*, **2011**, *1(2)*, 119-126.

6.   Petzet, A. Exploration and development frontiers report: World's frontier basins beckon exploration, *Oil & Gas Journal*, **2010**, *108(18)*, 34-37.

7.   Michael, D. (Ed.) (January 2011). Minor and Major Oil Spills in Indian waters (since 1982), *Blue Waters, Newsletter on Marine Environmental Security, XII(1)*, Retrieved from www.indiancoastguard.nic.in

8.   National Environment Engineering Research Institute. (2012) *Environmental Impact Assessment (EIA) Study on Pollution Due to Oil Spill and Other Hazardous Substances* (Interim Progress Report). Mumbai, India: Maharashtra Pollution Control Board.

9.   Kakatkar-Kulkarni, M. Oil spill off Mumbai coast as two cargo ships collide: India. http://coastalcare.org/2010/08/ (accessed December 8, 2015).

10.   Gholkar, D. (2005, September 3*)*. Darkness dawns on city's lighthouses. *Daily News and Analysis*. Retrieved from http://www.dnaindia.com

11.   Butcher Island, Maharashtra. http://www.netzone.com (accessed December 8, 2015).

12.   State of Conservation of the World Heritage Properties in the Asia-Pacific Region: India, Elephanta Caves. http://www.unesco.org (accessed December 8, 2015).

13.   Khan, S.M. Monitoring of oil spill contaminants in water samples from Elephanta Caves in Mumbai Oil Spill. http:// http://safarmdkhan.yolasite.com (accessed December 8, 2015).

14.   Mumbai Ship Collision a past: Environmental pollution is a bitter present. https://mapsofindia1.wordpress.com/2010/08/ (accessed December 8, 2015).

15.   City Map of Mumbai. http://www.mapsofindia.com (accessed December 8, 2015).

16.   NDTV Correspondent (2010, August 09). Mumbai Oil Spill stops but environmental threat remains. *NDTV* Retrieved from http://www.ndtv.com/india-news (accessed December 8, 2015).

17.   Michel, J.; Hayes, M.O. Weathering patterns of oil residues eight years after the Exxon Valdez oil spill, *Marine Pollution Bull.*, **1999**, *38*, 855-863.

18.   National Institute of Oceanography. (2010). *Impact of Hazardous Spillage of Oil And Hazardous Chemicals in Mumbai Bay Subsequent to Ship Collision on 7 August 2010, On Marine Ecology* (NIO/SP-68/2010, SSP2473). Mumbai, India: Maharashtra Pollution Control Board.

19.   Venkataraman, K. Marine Ecosystems of India. *Indian Journal of Environmental Education*, **2007**, *7*, 7-26.

20. Shinde, R.; Gawande, S. Oil Spills- A Threat to the Ocean Life by humans, *International Journal of Innovative Research in Science, Engineering and Technology*, **2015**, *4(9)*, 8257-8261.

21. Dunnet, G.; Crisp, D.; Conan, G.; Bourne, W. Oil Pollution and Seabird Populations [and Discussion]. *Philosophical Transactions of the Royal Society of London.* **1982**, *B 297(1087)*, 413–427.

22. Russell, J. 2000. Untold Seabird Mortality due to Marine Oil Pollution, Elements Online Environmental Magazine. http://www.elements.nb.ca/theme/fuels/janet/russell.htm (accessed December 8, 2015).

23. Definition of Luteinizing Hormone http://www.medicinenet.com/ (accessed December 8, 2015).

24. Dariusz M.B.; Kozlowski, R.; Gennady E. Z. Eds. *High Performance Elastomer Materials- An Engineering Approach*; Apple Academic Press: New Jersey, U.S.A., 2014.

25. Pneumatophore. (n.d.). *The American Heritage® Science Dictionary*. Retrieved December 08, 2015 from Dictionary.com website http://dictionary.reference.com/browse/pneumatophore

26. Larkin PA (1977) An epitaph for the concept of maximum sustained yield. *Transactions of the American Fisheries Society*, **1977**, *106*, 1–11; Walters, C.; Maguire, J. Lessons for stock assessment from the northern cod collapse, *Reviews in Fish Biology and Fisheries*, **1996**, *6*, 125–137.

27. Rebello, S. (2010, October 6). Vashi, Elephanta worst hit by oils spill. *The Hindustan Times.* Retrieved from http://www.hindustantimes.com

28. Staff Reporter (2010, October 7). Adult mangrove trees recovering well after oil spill: BNHS. *The Hindu.* Retrieved from www.thehindu.com

29. National Oceanic and Atmospheric Administration, U.S. Department of Commerce. Categories of Pollution: Point Source. http://oceanservice.noaa.gov/ (accessed December 9, 2015).

30. Lide, D. R., Ed. *CRC Handbook of Chemistry and Physics (90th ed.)*; CRC Press: Boca Raton, Florida, U.S.A., 2009.

31. Vollenweider, R.A.; Kerekes, J. Organization for Economic Co-operation and Development. (1982). *Eutrophication of waters. Monitoring, assessment and control. OECD Cooperative programme on monitoring of inland waters (Eutrophication control).* Paris: Environment Directorate; Vinebrooke, R.D.; Leavitt, P.R. Phytobenthos and phytoplankton as potential indicators of climate change in mountain lakes and ponds: a HPLC-based pigment approach. *J. N. Am. Benthol. Soc.* **1999**, *18(1)*, 15-33.

32. Thurman, H. V. *Introductory Oceanography*; Prentice Hall College: New Jersey, USA, 1997.

33. Kennish, M.J. Practical Handbook of Marine and Estuarine Pollution; CRC Press: New York, U.S.A., 1997.

34. Macrobenthos definition. http://www.science-dictionary.com (accessed December 9, 2015).

35. Worthington, D. *Dictionary of Environmental Health*; Taylor and Francis: U.K., 2004.

36. American Public Health Association (APHA). *Standard Methods for the Examination of Water and Wastewater (19th ed.)*; APHA: Washington, DC, U.S.A., 1995.

37. Doyle, M. P.; Erickson, M.C. 2006. Closing the door on the *fecal coliform* assay. *Microbe.* **2006**, *4(1)*, 162-163.

38. Thiel, H. (1982) "Standing Stock." In *Encyclopedia of Earth Sciences*. (19, pp. 792-794). U.S.A.: Springer.

39. Metcalf, R.L. (2000) "Insect Control." In *Ullmann's Encyclopedia of Industrial Chemistry* Weinheim, Germany: Wiley-VCH.

40. Lal, B. V.; Fortune, K., Ed. *The Pacific Islands: An Encyclopedia*; University of Hawaii Press: Honolulu, U.S.A., 2000.

41. Pandey, I.P.; Rai, N. (2011). Impact and Assessment of Recent Oil Spills on Environment, *ONGC Bulletin. 45(1)*. Retrieved from http://nucssi.niscair.res.in

42. Brekke, C.; Solberg, A.H.S. Oil spill detection by satellite remote sensing, *Rem. Sens. Environ.*, **2005**, *95*, 1-13.

43. Jensen, J. R.; Halls, J. N.; Michel, J. A Systems Approach to Environmental Sensitivity Index (ESI) Mapping for Oil Spill Contingency Planning and Response. *Photogrammetric Engineering & Remote Sensing*, **1998**, *64(10)*, 1003-1014.

44. Exxon Valdez Oil Spill, Office of Response and Restoration, National Oceanic and Atmospheric Administration. http://response.restoration.noaa.gov (accessed December 9, 2015); Steiner, R. Lessons from Exxon Valdez, 25 years later. http://www.greenpeace.org (accessed December 9, 2015).

45. Oil Spill CleanUp Technology. Patent and patent applications archived. https://web.archive.org/web (accessed December 9, 2015).

46. Kasai, Y.; Kishira, H.; Sasaki, T.; Syutsubo, K.; Watanabe, K.; Harayama, S. Predominant Growth of *Alcanivorax* Strains in Oil-contaminated and Nutrient-supplemented Sea Water. *Environmental Microbiology*, **2002**, *4(3)*, 141-47.

47. Oil and Natural Gas eating bacteria to clear-up spills, Oil and Gas Technology. http://www.oilandgastechnology.net (accessed December 9, 2015).

48. NCP Product Schedule (Products available for use on Oil Spills), United States Environment Protection Agency. http://www.epa.gov/emergency-response (accessed December 9, 2015).

49. Emergency Response: Responding to Oil Spills, Office of Response and Restoration, National Oceanic and Atmospheric Administration. http://response.restoration.noaa.gov (accessed December 9, 2015)

50. Dispersants, International Tanker Operators Pollution Federation Limited. http://www.itopf.com/knowledge-resources/documents-guides/clean-up-techniques/dispersants/ (accessed December 9, 2015).

51. Patel, P.V.; Mehta, M.J. The risks, impacts and mitigation option for accidental oil spills. *Int. J. Advanced Research in Science, Engineering and Management,* **2015,** *1(5),* 1-6.

52. Pezeshki, S. R., Hester, M. W., Lin, Q. & Nyman, J. A. The effects of oil spill clean-up on dominant US Gulf coast marsh macrophytes: a review. *Environmental Pollution,* **2000,** *108,* 129-139.

53. The Editors of Encyclopedia Britannica, Oil Spill. (2015). In *Encyclopedia Britannica.* Retrieved from http://www.britannica.com/science/oil-spill#ref279919 (accessed December 9, 2015).

54. Fountain, H. (2010, June 24). Advances in Oil Spill Cleanup Lag Since Valdez. *New York Times.* Retrieved from http://www.nytimes.com/

55. Iseppi, V. Oil Spill Cleanup, BARBER. http://www.hbarber.com/Cleaners/SurfRake/applications/oil-spill-cleanup-equipment.html (accessed December 9, 2015).

56. Chaddha, M. (2010, August 23). Oil-zapping bacteria employed to clean up Mumbai Oil soaked beaches. http://cleantechnica.com (accessed December 9, 2015).

APPENDIX A

Table 1: Minor and Major Oil Spills in Indian Waters (Since 1982) [7]

S. No.	Date	Quantity and Type of Spill (Tons)	Location	Spilled By
1.	1982	Not Assessed	West Coast	Sagar Vikas
2.	24/10/88	1000	Bombay Harbor	Lajpat Rai
3.	1989	Not Assessed	West Coast	SEDCO 252
4.	1989	5500/Diesel Oil	795 nm SW of Bombay	MT Puppy
5.	04/8/1989	Not Assessed	Bombay Harbor	ONGC Tanker
6.	29/8/1989	Not Assessed	Saurashtra coast	Merchant ship
7.	29/8/1989	Not Assessed	Bombay Harbor	Unknown
8.	22/3/1990	Not Assessed	NW of Cochin	Merchant ship
9.	07/9/1991	692/FO	Gulf of Mannar	MT Jayabola
10.	14/11/1991	40000/Crude	Bombay High	MT Zakir Hussain
11.	22/2/1992	Tanker wash	40 NM S. of New Moore Island	Unknown
12.	2/4/1992	1000/Crude	54 NM west of Kochi	MT Homi Bhabha
13.	16/8/1992	1060/SKO	Madras Harbor	MT Albert Ekka

Table 1: Minor and Major Oil Spills in Indian Waters (Since 1982) [7] (contd.)

S. No.	Date	Quantity and Type of Spill (Tons)	Location	Spilled By
14.	17/11/1992	300/FO	Bombay Harbor	MV Moon River
15.	21/1/1993	40000	Off Nicobar Islands	Maersk Navigator
16.	28/1/1993	NK/Crude	Off Narsapur	ONGC shore rig at Kumarada
17.	29/4/1993	110/Crude	Bombay Harbor	MT Nand Shivchand
18.	10/5/1993	90/FO	Bhavnagar	MV Celelia
19.	17/5/1993	6000/Crude	Bombay High	BHN Riser pipe rupture
20.	02/8/1993	260/FO	Off New Mangalore	MV Challenge
21.	01/10/1993	90/Crude	Cochin Harbor	MT Nand Shiv Chand
22.	12/5/1994	1600/Crude	Off Sacromento Pt.	Innovative-1
23.	12/5/1994	Not Assessed/FO	360 NM SW of Porbandar	MV Stolidi
24.	05/6/1994	1025/Crude	Off Aguada Lt	MV Sea Transporter
25.	20/7/1994	100/FO	Bombay Harbor	MV Maharshi Dayanand

Table 1: Minor and Major Oil Spills in Indian Waters (Since 1982) [7] (contd.)

S. No.	Date	Quantity and Type of Spill (Tons)	Location	Spilled By
26.	27/11/1994	288/HO	Off Madras	MV Sagar
27.	26/3/1995	200/Diesel	Off Vizag	Dredger Mandovi-2
28.	24/9/1995	Not Assessed/FO	Off Dwarka	MC Pearl
29.	13/11/1995	Tanker wash	Eliot beach, Madras	Unknown
30.	21/15/1996	370 FO	Hooghly River	MV Prem Tista
31.	16/6/1996	120/FO	Off Prongs, Mumbai	MV Tupi Buzios
32.	18/6/1996	132/FO	Off Bandra, Mumbai	MV Zien Don
33.	18/6/1996	128/FO	Off Karanja, Mumbai	MV Indian Prosperity
34.	23/6/1996	110/FO	Off Worli, Mumbai	MV Romanska
35.	16/8/1996	124/FO	Malabar Coast	MV Al-Hadi
36.	25/1/1997	Tank wash	Kakinada Coast	Unknown
37.	19/6/1997	210/FO	Off Prongs Lt, Mumbai	MV Arcadia Pride
38.	19/6/1997	Not Assessed	Hooghly River	MV Green Opal

Table 1: Minor and Major Oil Spills in Indian Waters (Since 1982) (contd.)

S. No.	Date	Quantity and Type of Spill (Tons)	Location	Spilled By
39.	14/9/1997	Naptha, Diesel Petrol	Vizag	HPC Refinery
40.	02/8/1997	70/FO	Off Mumbai	MV Sea Empress
41.	10/3/1998	Gas Leak	Bombay High	Drill Rig Noble
42.	12/5/1998	Gas Leak	Bombay High	Bombay High platform
43.	01/6/1998	20/Crude	Off Vadinar	Vadinar, SBM
44.	09/6/1998	Not Assessed	Off Porbandar	Ocean Barge
45.	09/6/1998	Not Assessed	Off Veraval	Ocean Pacific
46.	08/7/1999	500/FO	Mul Dwarka	MV Pacific Acadian
47.	19/7/2000	Not Assessed	Off Sagar Island	MV Prime Value
48.	8/9/2000	Not Assessed	Off Fort Aguada	MV River Princess
49.	17/12/2000	1/FO	Bombay Harbor	MV Stonswall Jackson
50.	08/6/2001	Not Assessed	Vadinar Gulf of Kutch	Not known
51.	10/7/2001	1305/Diesel Oil	Hooghly river	MV Lucnam
52.	23/09/2002	Not Assessed	Off Pt. Calimare 220 NM	MV HIDERBAHY
53.	29/04/2003	2000 L of Arab light crude oil	05 miles off Kochi	MT BR AMBEDKAR

Table 1: Minor and Major Oil Spills in Indian Waters (Since 1982) (contd.)

S. No.	Date	Quantity and Type of Spill (Tons)	Location	Spilled By
54.	09/05/2003	2000/Naptha	Mumbai harbor (SW of West Colaba Point)	MT UPCO_III
55.	18/05/2003	145/FFO	Off Haldia	MV SEGITEGA BIRU
56.	10/08/2003	300/Crude Oil	ONGC Rig (BHN)	URAN Pipe line
57.	28/02/2004	01/Crude Oil	36 inches ONGC pipeline at MPT Oil Jetty (Tata Jetty- OPL PIRPAU)	During crude oil transfer from Jawahar Dweep to ONGC-Trombay through 36" pipe
58.	01/10/2004	500 to 600 L	Berth- MPT- 8 Goa	During oil transfer
59.	23/03/2005	110	Off Goa (Aguada Lt)	MV Maritime Wisdom off Aguada Lt.
60.	27/07/2005	80	Fire taken place on oil platform off Bombay High	BHN Platform Bombay High

Table 1: Minor and Major Oil Spills in Indian Waters (Since 1982) (contd.)

S. No.	Date	Quantity and Type of Spill (Tons)	Location	Spilled By
61.	30/08/2005	08	Sunken Ship off Tuticorin	MV IIDA
62.	21/04/2006	90	Sunken ship off Goa	INS Prahar
63.	06/05/2006	Minor spill (less than 100 L)	Sunken Tug Off Pt. Calimer Tamil Nadu	DCI Tug-IV
64.	30/05/2006	70 tons of FFO	Grounded off Karawar Port	MV Ocean Seraya
65.	14/08/2006	4500	Outside Indian EEZ near Andaman & Nicobar Islands	MV Bright Artemis & MV Amar
66.	15/10/2007	13.9/FO	Off Jakhau	MV Star Lelkanger & barge Dhan Lakshmi due to collision
67.	17/10/2007	Not assessed Kakinada	South Yanam Beach, oil rigs	Oil drifted to shore from
68.	19/07/2009	50 L	Off Mangalore	MV Asian Forest
69.	06/08/2009 to 13/08/2009	Approx 200 tons (Oil debris wash-off on the shorelines)	South Gujarat and Maharashtra Coast (Western India)	Not established

Table 1: Minor and Major Oil Spills in Indian Waters (Since 1982) (contd.)

S. No.	Date	Quantity and Type of Spill (Tons)	Location	Spilled By
70.	09/09/2009	200-500 L	Paradip Port Anchorage	MV Black Rose
71.	02/01/2010	05 tons	Off South Chennai	Not known
72.	12/04/2010	08-10 tons	Gopalpur (Orissa)	MV Malvika
73.	20/07/2010	80 tons	Panna Offshore, Near Panna SBM	PMT Joint Venture
74.	07/08/2010	700 tons (approx)	Mumbai Harbor	MC Chitra
75.	15/08/2010	20 KL oil removed from the ship	Eastern side of Kavaratti Island	MV Nanda Aprajita
76.	23/11/2010	12 tons	Off Hugli Point	Collision between MV Tiger Spring and MV Green Valley

ABOUT THE AUTHOR

Dr. Sonali Bhandari is a New Delhi based Professor of Chemistry and Environmental Sciences and the Head of Department of Chemistry at Shree Guru Gobind Singh Tricentenary University, Gurugram, India. She enjoys listening to music, reading books, travelling and going to the theatre. Raising awareness about the environment among the general public is her passion.